Cultivating Spiritual Growth

Striving for Maturity in Christ

Conrad Mbewe

Reformation Heritage Books
Grand Rapids, Michigan

Reformation Heritage Books
3070 29th St. SE
Grand Rapids, MI 49512
616-977-0889
orders@heritagebooks.org
www.heritagebooks.org

Printed in the United States of America
24 25 26 27 28 29/10 9 8 7 6 5 4 3 2 1

Library of Congress Cataloging-in-Publication Data

Names: Mbewe, Conrad, author.
Title: Cultivating spiritual growth : striving for maturity in Christ / Conrad Mbewe.
Description: Grand Rapids, Michigan : Reformation Heritage Books, 2024.
Identifiers: LCCN 2024018601 (print) | LCCN 2024018602 (ebook) | ISBN 9798886861037 (hardback) | ISBN 9798886861044 (epub)
Subjects: LCSH: Spiritual life—Christianity.
Classification: LCC BV4501.3 .M3188 2024 (print) | LCC BV4501.3 (ebook) | DDC 248.4—dc23/eng/20240515
LC record available at https://lccn.loc.gov/2024018601
LC ebook record available at https://lccn.loc.gov/2024018602

Contents

Introduction

Where there is life, there is change. However, for growth to occur there must be deliberate effort. Two people can be born in the same family and be raised together, but if one person is not taking good care of his own health, you will discover that he struggles to grow and may even become sick and weak. What is true in the natural realm is also true in the spiritual. Two individuals can come to Christ within the same year. Ten or twenty years later, one of them will still be in spiritual diapers, while the other is a mature adult in Christ, having a fruitful and impactful spiritual life in the church and in the world. Often, the difference is in how much effort these individuals have put into their own spiritual growth.

A lot of believers treat salvation like fire insurance—in this case, hellfire insurance. They are happy that they have it and are going to heaven. The fact that they need to grow does not occur to them. Worse still, they do not realize it is their responsibility to ensure that they grow spiritually. Therefore, we have so few believers who manifest mature adulthood in Christ.

This is what the writer of the letter to the Hebrews was concerned about. He wrote,

> Having been perfected, He became the author of eternal salvation to all who obey Him, called by God as High Priest "according to the order of Melchizedek," of whom we have much to say, and hard to explain, since you have become dull of hearing.

For though by this time you ought to be teachers, you need someone to teach you again the first principles of the oracles of God; and you have come to need milk and not solid food. For everyone who partakes only of milk is unskilled in the word of righteousness, for he is a babe. But solid food belongs to those who are of full age, that is, those who by reason of use have their senses exercised to discern both good and evil.

Therefore, leaving the discussion of the elementary principles of Christ, let us go on to perfection. (Heb. 5:9–6:1)

This common lack of understanding regarding the necessity of spiritual growth has compelled me to undertake this study of 2 Peter 1. In this chapter, Peter describes how steady spiritual growth results in a fruitful and godly life: "For if these things are yours and abound, you will be neither barren nor unfruitful in the knowledge of our Lord Jesus Christ" (2 Peter 1:8). Putting it positively, if you have these qualities in an ever-increasing measure, they will make you effective and fruitful in your Christian life. In short, you must keep on growing. Nothing can be clearer than that!

PART 1

The Indicatives
of Spiritual Growth

CHAPTER 1

You Have a Faith of Equal Standing

Simon Peter, a bondservant and apostle of Jesus Christ,

To those who have obtained like precious faith with us by the righteousness of our God and Savior Jesus Christ:

Grace and peace be multiplied to you in the knowledge of God and of Jesus our Lord.
—2 PETER 1:1–2

Most African youths enjoy playing soccer. They play this game at home and in schools, in the villages and in the big cities. However, when it comes to watching and following big league soccer, most of them are glued to the popular teams in Europe. Teams such as Manchester United, Real Madrid, FC Barcelona, FC Bayern Munich, Manchester City, Chelsea, Arsenal, and Liverpool are household names across the continent. As the soccer season nears its end, some fans are full of excitement because their teams are performing very well, while other supporters are deflated because of their team's lackluster performance. Yet each soccer season began with a level playing field, so to speak. The teams have no goals and no points on their records. Their coaches and managers have had similar opportunities to assemble the best team possible.

The Christian race, which is another way of referring to the Christian life, is also like that. We all begin with the same foundation of faith in the Lord Jesus Christ. No one has a starting advantage that ensures he or she will become a spiritual giant compared to their friends. This is what the apostle Peter seeks to emphasize in the salutation that begins his letter.

Ancient letters often began with the author's self-introduction. This was because they were written on scrolls. You could not peep at the end to see who had written the letter to you, as is the case with modern letters. Thus, knowing who wrote the letter and then to whom he was writing from the very onset made a lot of sense as you began to unroll the scroll. As with most apostolic epistles, within the salutation you can sense what was on the author's mind as he began writing the letter. It is discernible even in this epistle. As we have already noted, Peter wanted the recipients of his letter to know that all Christians have a faith that is of equal standing—whether they are apostles or ordinary run-of-the-mill believers. This knowledge is vital if we are going to find a biblical answer as to why some believers are spiritual giants and others are not. We must start by acknowledging that we all start on the same footing—with precisely the same faith.

The Writer

Who is this writer who tells us we have a faith of equal standing with him? He identifies himself as "Simeon Peter, a bondservant and apostle of Jesus Christ." The apostle Peter is better known as Simon Peter. Some English versions use Simon, while others use Simeon (the Hebrew variation) in the salutation of 2 Peter. This is because no copy machines existed when the Bible was being reproduced in the years of the early church. Someone would dictate what was on the original document while a number of other people would copy what was being read onto their own documents. It is very possible that in copying what was being dictated, some ended up writing the Greek name, Simon, while others ended up writing the Hebrew name, Simeon. What matters to us is that the man introducing himself is the same person we know who walked with Jesus Christ and learned from Him firsthand.

This Simeon or Simon Peter referred to himself as a servant and apostle of Jesus Christ. The Greek word for *servant* is not *diakonos* (which literally means "servant") but *doulos* (which literally means "slave"). The word refers to someone who has no personal rights because those rights have been given over to another human being who is the master. Whereas a servant could resign his job, a slave could not do that because he was owned by his master. His entire life was to be lived under the dictates of another person. This is how Peter understood his relationship with the Lord Jesus Christ. He was a slave of Christ. And that is what we all are as Christians. We do not negotiate with Him about what He wants to do with our lives. Whatever He says, we must do. Our job is to say, "What shall I do, Lord?" (Acts 22:10). That is an important test of whether we have genuinely become Christians.

Peter also introduced himself as an apostle of Jesus Christ. The word *apostle* means a "sent out one." He was sent out by the Lord to do His will. Whereas being a slave of Jesus Christ is true of all who are Christians, being an apostle is not. This is because, strictly speaking, apostleship was limited to the twelve individuals who saw and heard the Lord Jesus Christ and were the first recipients of the Great Commission (Matt. 28:16–20). All these twelve have since died. They laid the foundation for the Christian faith on which the rest of us are now building, according to the gifts God has given us (Eph. 2:20).

To the apostles was revealed the nature of salvation in Jesus Christ. Jesus Himself had spent no less than three years discipling them so that they would know the only way of salvation and how God wants us to live as New Testament believers. Before Jesus went back to heaven, He said to them, "No longer do I call you servants, for a servant does not know what his master is doing; but I have called you friends, for all things that I heard from My Father I have made known to you" (John 15:15). Over three years the whole plan of salvation had been shared with the apostles in word and deed as they observed and heard the Son of God. It is important to recognize this from the very onset of this study because it means that what we learn about spiritual growth from the apostle Peter is not simply a list of pragmatic ideas. This is the very nature of salvation as it was revealed to him and the other apostles by our Lord Jesus Christ. It is how Jesus Himself expects us to grow spiritually. If we do not follow what Peter is telling us to do, we disobey our Lord—we disobey God. And we do so to our own spiritual peril. Peter wrote not only as our fellow slave (in total obedience to the Master) but also as one entrusted with the very words of God. We must listen to him!

The Readers

Peter states that he was writing to individuals who had a faith equal to his own through the righteousness of Jesus. Our text says, "To those who have obtained like precious faith with us by the righteousness of our God and Savior Jesus Christ" (2 Peter 1:1). Who were these people? If it was the apostle Paul's letter to the Romans we would have said, "They were the believers in the church in Rome." Similarly, if it was the apostle Paul's letter to the Corinthians, we would have said, "The recipients are the Christians who make up the church in Corinth." This is because Paul mentions the recipients at the very start of those letters. Peter's epistle is referred to as a general epistle because it does not state who the specific recipients were. It is in the same category as the epistles of James and John.

Later, in this second epistle, Peter writes, "Beloved, I now write to you this second epistle" (2 Peter 3:1). This implies that we could get some clues about his audience if we look at the salutation in his first epistle. There we read, "Peter, an apostle of Jesus Christ, the pilgrims of the Dispersion in Pontus, Galatia, Cappadocia, Asia, and Bithynia" (1 Peter 1:1). By elect exiles, Peter was speaking about Christians who had been dispersed by persecution. He mentions the regions where most of them had been scattered—Pontus, Galatia, Cappadocia, Asia, and Bithynia. We would be right to conclude that he had these same people in mind as he was writing this second epistle. You will find that the theme of suffering is very strong in both epistles. The recipients of both letters were under intense persecution for their faith. Yet Peter was not only counseling them about how to stand in the midst of suffering. He specifically begins this second letter with an appeal for them to grow up spiritually. As he writes later in this first chapter, spiritual growth will keep them effective and fruitful in their Christian lives, despite persecution. It will also prevent them from falling and will ensure that their entrance into heaven is richly rewarded.

Peter describes the recipients of his second epistle as those who have obtained a faith of equal standing with his. The Greek phrase *lanchano*, translated "have obtained," is a little deeper than the English rendering suggests. It means to receive and is in the past tense. These believers have received this faith already. It is completely in their possession. Second, the phrase suggests that the believers were merely recipients of this faith. The giver of this faith determined whom He gave it to; God was sovereign in dispensing this faith. It is interesting that two other places where this Greek phrase is used in the New Testament refer to people casting lots (Luke 1:9; John 19:24). Like the modern equivalent of playing dice, the number you end up with is totally out of your control. It is dependent on the absolutely sovereign will of God. When Peter uses this phrase, he is making the point that it was not their decision that gave them this faith. It was an act of God. He chose them in eternity to be the recipients of this precious faith, and in time He gave this gift to them and not to others. That is why in his first epistle the apostle Peter called them elect.

Christians need to be grateful to God for every part of our salvation since our faith has been given to us as a gift of God (Eph. 2:8). We were not the primary mover—God was. We are not believers because of our cleverness or because some of us were brought up in a Christian home. God in His sovereignty brought this about. He chose us. We are simply recipients of His super-abounding grace.

According to Peter, what did the scattered believers obtain? It was a "like precious faith." The faith spoken about here is not referring to the doctrines of Christianity. It is not what you believe but rather the instrument by which you believe. When the word *faith* has the definite article preceding it (i.e., the faith), it normally refers to the body of teaching that is believed in. However, when the definite article is missing (i.e., a faith), it normally refers to the element in us that trusts and believes. "The faith" is objective and is external to us, while "faith" is subjective and resides in our hearts. In this case, the apostle Peter is referring to the latter, which is the God-given ability to lay hold of the truth about Him. He is making the point that this element is the same in all of us—whether you are living today or you were living in the first century. It is of equal value, of equal honor, and of equal preciousness. There is no difference. We have the same faith.

What is even more amazing is that when Peter speaks about this faith that we share, he includes himself as an apostle. Remember his introduction: "Simeon Peter, a bondservant and apostle of Jesus Christ, to those who have obtained like precious faith with us." Whether Peter was referring to the apostles only or the apostles and other believers, it certainly included him as an apostle. We may differ in gifts, but God gives us the same saving faith by which we trust in His Son, the Lord Jesus Christ, for our salvation. In that sense, the apostles were not a different category of believers. The same Holy Spirit who opened the spiritual eyes of Peter and Paul is the one who opened the spiritual eyes of all the believers to whom Peter was writing. So, why should there be a difference?

The basis of our obtaining an equal faith as the apostles is that the same price was paid for our salvation, and we are clothed in the same righteousness. Peter writes, "To those who have obtained like precious faith with us by the righteousness of our God and Savior Jesus Christ." The price that was paid for the faith that was in the heart of Peter is the same price that was paid for the faith of all true believers. Jesus obtained a faultless righteousness by His perfectly blameless life on earth and then He paid for our sins by His death on the cross.

This is an indicative, a statement of fact about all believers. They have obtained a faith of equal standing with the apostles by the righteousness of our God and Savior Jesus Christ. Sadly, if you looked at many believers today you would not think so. We may be more in number today compared to the believers in the first century, but the spirituality we see in the early church is largely lacking nowadays. First-century believers were under intense persecution, but they stood the test of time. They impacted their world by their lives. They were being thrown to wild beasts to be eaten alive as part of entertainment in their society.

We need to stop reading the book of Acts as if we were watching a movie. In movies, people are acting to entertain us. Those superheroes like Superman, Spiderman, and Wonder Woman are not real. We know that. We do not even try to imitate them because we know they are acting. Yet the people we read about in the Bible were real people, with weaknesses and frailties similar to our own. They were going through life in the real world the way we do. They went through the same trials that we go through—if not worse. As we read about them overcoming the world, we should know that the faith that upheld them is precisely the same faith that is in us. Remember, it is of equal value, of equal honor, and of equal preciousness. There is no difference between what God did in them and what God has done in us.

It is easy to give excuses for our indolence, ineffectiveness, and unfruitfulness when we are comparing ourselves with the people around us. Our generation can be very easy on itself. We explain away our lack of growth and fruitfulness by pointing to the pressure of work and the difficult economic circumstances in which we live. On judgment day, when our eyes are opened to what other believers went through to live for Christ in their own day, our excuses will be too lame to be mentioned in the presence of God. Although we have obtained a "like precious faith," they added to theirs the qualities of virtue, knowledge, self-control, steadfastness, godliness, brotherly kindness, and love, while we are content to simply cruise along in our spiritual journey to heaven.

The Greeting

The apostle Peter greeted the believers he was writing to with a prayer: "Grace and peace be multiplied to you in the knowledge of God and of Jesus our Lord." This is not a uniquely Petrine greeting. The apostle Paul begins almost all his epistles by wishing God's grace and peace on the recipients of his letters (see, e.g., Rom. 1:7; 1 Cor. 1:3; 2 Cor. 1:2; Gal. 1:3). Sometimes he also adds in God's mercy for good measure (1 Tim. 1:2; 2 Tim. 1:2). We can rightly say that this was a normal form of apostolic greeting. The believers Peter was writing to already had God's grace and peace. His grace was the source of their salvation and His peace was the resulting fruit. Yet Peter prayed for more grace and peace. He wanted these blessings of God to be multiplied to his brethren. This could happen in only one way—through their saving and sanctifying knowledge of God and of His Son.

God's grace is His unmerited favor on those who deserve the exact opposite. We deserve God's wrath, but instead He favors us. In this salutation, Peter prays that this unmerited favor of God may be on these elect exiles in superabundance. As we have already said, peace is the fruit of this grace. You know that God has been gracious to you because He fills you with His own peace. The two are related as cause and effect. Everyone who is saved from sin will possess both. They should be able to say, "God was gracious in saving me from my sin, and He gave me a peace that is beyond understanding."

In praying that God's people should have this grace and peace in superabundance, Peter is asking that they may know the God-given energy that results in spiritual sustenance and growth. It is what the apostle Paul spoke about when he wrote, "Therefore, having been justified by faith, we have peace with God through our Lord Jesus Christ, through whom also we have access by faith into this grace in which we stand, and rejoice in hope of the glory of God" (Rom. 5:1–2). Justification by faith results in peace with God and places believers in a context where He deals graciously with them in an ongoing way, which results in their abiding joy and defiant hope. This is the essence of Peter's prayer in his salutation.

It is this divine energy, mediated by the Holy Spirit, that enables us to gallop along spiritually where others get stuck in the mud. Listen to the apostle Paul again: "Not only that, but we also glory in tribulations, knowing that tribulation produces perseverance; and perseverance, character; and character, hope. Now hope does not disappoint, because the love of God has been poured out in our hearts by the Holy Spirit who was given to us" (Rom. 5:3–5). This is what Peter wanted to see in these persecuted believers. He desired that they would rejoice in their suffering and grow because of it.

In one sense, then, this is what we utterly depend on to make progress in our Christian lives. We need the abiding presence of the Holy Spirit to give us more and more of His grace and peace as we face the challenges of each new day. This is what will take us from being thumb-sucking spiritual toddlers to becoming mature adults in Christ despite the adverse circumstances we find ourselves in. This is what will take us from swimming in the shallow end of our own domestic pool to swimming in the ocean of life without sinking.

Peter says that this grace and peace is multiplied "in the knowledge of God and of Jesus our Lord." Our God truly is a trinitarian God! When we encounter one person of the Godhead, it's not long before we notice that we are dealing indirectly with the other two. We find the same here. In his greeting, Peter says, "in the knowledge," but in verse 3 he says, "through the knowledge" (see also 2 Peter 2:20). Grace and peace are mediated to us by the Holy Spirit, but they come because of the knowledge of God and of Jesus our Lord. This is both the doctrinal and experiential knowledge that our faith grasps at the point of our salvation and in the process of our growth and sanctification. By implication, the more knowledge we have, the deeper our experience of spiritual victory. This foreshadows the reason Peter will later urge believers to add knowledge to their virtue and faith (v. 5). We will deal with this more in the next chapter. Suffice to say for now, you cannot experience God's abiding grace and peace in superabundance while living in the shallow end of knowing Him. You need to grow in your knowledge of God.

We all have a faith of equal standing with the apostles and the Christians in the early church. We all start in the same place with the same faith. What makes the difference in maturity between you and other believers is how seriously you take your spiritual growth. Are you deliberately striving to know God more? Have you carved out time for church services and Bible study? Do you take time to read Scripture and good Christian books? I am encouraging you to look again at your spiritual disciplines because the grace and peace you experience in your Christian life is determined largely by your experience of knowing God. This will not happen automatically. You must be intentional and make time for it.

CHAPTER 2

You Have All You Need to Grow Up

His divine power has given to us all things that pertain to life and godliness, through the knowledge of Him who called us by glory and virtue, by which have been given to us exceedingly great and precious promises, that through these you may be partakers of the divine nature, having escaped the corruption that is in the world through lust.

—2 PETER 1:3–4

A few years ago, with the full blessing of my wife, I bought myself a full-body workout machine. With it, I can exercise any muscle in my entire body—from the soles of my feet to the crown of my head—and work my way to optimum physical health. I do not need to be out of shape while that piece of equipment is in my house. As I look at pictures of men with six-pack abs, I know that everything I need to achieve that kind of body has been provided for in that one piece of equipment. All I need is instruction on how to use it and the self-discipline to put it to good use. That is what Peter is telling us in 2 Peter 1:3–4. We have no excuse for lacking in fruitfulness, because everything we need to reach peak spiritual fitness has been provided by the Lord Jesus Christ.

His Divine Power Has Given Us All Things

The apostle Peter says that God's power gives us everything we need to attain and sustain our spiritual life and godliness (v. 3). The original Greek puts it this way: "All things that pertain to life and godliness, his divine power has granted to us." Peter is not emphasizing the source of what is given to us but rather the gift we receive from that source. We have received "all things"—absolutely everything we need. This is mind-blowing. As you think about your own spiritual growth and admire those in your church whose maturity shines like the sun on a cloudless summer day, it is vital that you realize you, too, can be like that because God has denied you nothing for this journey. What you need to sustain your spiritual life and grow into maturity has already been granted to you by the power of God.

We were once spiritually dead and could do nothing for ourselves to merit God's favor and to bring us into fellowship with Him. The apostle Paul says, "And you He made alive, who were dead in trespasses and sins, in which you once walked according to the course of this world, according to the prince of the power of the air, the spirit who now works in the sons of disobedience, among whom also we all once conducted ourselves in the lusts of our flesh, fulfilling the desires of the flesh and of the mind, and were by nature children of wrath, just as the others" (Eph. 2:1–3). God's own power brought us to life, and it requires His power to sustain that life in us. This life radiates godliness in us, and as a result we become godly too. The apostle Peter could therefore write, "His divine power has given to us all things that pertain to life and godliness." The life and godliness being spoken about here are not two independent items. This is because the spiritual life we get from God is a moral life, one that transforms us from the inside out. It is a life that forms godliness in us.

Godliness refers to an attitude of desiring to please God in everything you do—in your eating, your pleasure, your personal relationships, your work, your school, and even your churchgoing. You are gripped by the fact that God must be honored and worshiped in all things. Consequently, you are willing to sacrifice so much that other people are chasing after because your eye is on one thing—all you want is to please God. That is godliness.

Godliness is not natural. In the apostle Paul's description of our state before conversion, we were spiritually dead and were slaves of Satan, the world, and our own fallen nature. In that threefold enslavement, godly desires were impossible. Paul wrote to the Romans, "The carnal mind is enmity against God; for it is not subject to the law of God, nor indeed can be. So then, those who are in the flesh cannot please God" (Rom. 8:7–8). We are self-centered until the regenerating power of God makes us alive in Christ Jesus. In regeneration, the seed of righteousness is planted in our hearts. This gives us new God-centered desires, which previously were impossible. The divine power of the Lord Jesus Christ does that to us. That is why we call Him Savior. He truly saves us from our spiritual death and sin.

Peter is careful in the way he describes what God's power has done for us and in us. He says, "His divine power has given to us." This suggests something granted freely, something we never worked for. It also suggests a complete transaction. It has been given to us and is now in our hands.

If you are truly converted to Christ, you should realize that God has already given everything that you need to sustain your spiritual life and to secure godliness. The initial transformation you experienced at your conversion was only the start of an ascent that is fueled by the Holy Spirit. You should no longer be taxiing on the runway. You ought to be ascending through the clouds! Those Christians whose godly lives you admire have reached spiritual heights by the power of our Lord Jesus Christ. It is not due to something unique about them that may not be true of you. The work of God in their souls is now being manifested in their outward lives.

Through Our Knowledge of Jesus Christ

The apostle Peter proceeds to describe how the power of God works in our lives. It is "through the knowledge of Him who called us by glory and virtue" (2 Peter 1:3). Peter already referred to this knowledge of the Lord Jesus Christ in his greeting when he wrote in the previous verse, "Grace and peace be multiplied to you in the knowledge of God and of Jesus our Lord" (2 Peter 1:2). Was he simply repeating himself? No, this time he is emphasizing the glory and excellence that Jesus is calling His people to. He did not want his readers to miss the fact that the one through whom they grow into spiritual maturity has called them to that maturity Himself. We will look at this shortly. For now, let us observe the need for knowledge in the Christian faith.

Christianity hangs on our foundational knowledge of the person and work of Jesus Christ. It is the way in which we come to faith. We cannot become Christians if we do not know the person and work of the Lord Jesus (John 17:3). That is why when missionaries go all over the world to establish the Christian faith, they go to tell people about Jesus. Unless their hearers come to know this Jesus and put their trust in Him, they cannot be saved. Spiritual life and godliness begin with knowing Christ in a saving way.

Spiritual development and its attendant godliness comes from growing in this knowledge. When your knowledge becomes stale, so do your spiritual life and godliness. This is why when Peter begins to urge believers to grow in verse 5, he urges them to add virtue (or excellence) to their faith and then to add knowledge to their virtue. We will learn more about this knowledge in a later chapter. For now, it is important simply to recognize that there is no true spiritual growth where the knowledge of Jesus Christ is not the driving force.

In the natural world, parents know that children need to eat to grow. Thus, they are careful about eating times. They want their children to have a balanced diet and good nutrition. When a child falls sick and loses their appetite, parents never give up. They realize that it is by eating that the child will gain strength to fight illness and repair the body's cells. So they do their best to ensure that the child still eats. With time, as the child gets better, their appetite picks up and life goes back to normal. Growth is secured again.

What is true in the natural world is also true in the spiritual. We need to keep feeding the mind with truth in order to grow. Sin causes a loss of spiritual appetite, which results in a loss of interest in knowing more about the things of our great God and redeemer, Jesus Christ. You start giving excuses for not reading Scripture and for missing church services and Bible studies. The truth is that your soul is sick. In fact, that is when you need your Bible even more. We must keep encouraging ourselves to continue in the knowledge of our Savior. As we are restored spiritually, our appetite returns, and we want to learn more about Christ. We want to be refreshed by this knowledge, which further strengthens our godliness. The energy realized from this causes us to be fruitful as believers.

We observed earlier that in referring to the knowledge of our Lord Jesus Christ twice within the first three verses, Peter is not simply repeating himself. Rather, he is emphasizing the call of Jesus Christ on our lives. It is a call toward His own glory and excellence. Let us now consider this more closely.

Different versions of the Bible translate this slightly differently. Some versions say, "He has called us *by* his own glory and virtue/ excellence," while others say, "He has called us *to* his own glory and virtue/excellence." The Greek grammatical construction can go either way. The point Peter seems to be making is that the glory and excellence of Jesus is meant to cause us to seek higher spiritual ground. This is what He has called us toward by the very nature of His being. When we begin relating to Him, we realize that we must pursue becoming more like Him.

Think of it this way: Whether you are applying for a job at an automotive repair garage or at the central bank of your country, one of the questions you will ask yourself is how you should dress for the interview. The invitation for the interview does not need to tell you how to dress. You will think in terms of "dressing for the job." Most likely, for the interview at the garage you will go in something that is business casual or even in blue overalls, but for an interview at the top bank of your country you will be in very smart professional attire. The glory and excellence of the bank has made you reach for your sharpest clothing. Beyond considering how you should dress, you will also want to know more about the company and ask yourself,

What value will I bring? Let us use the bank as our example. You will increase your knowledge of the bank by reading whatever you can get your hands on that summarizes its history, its operations, its management, and so on. As you expose yourself to all this, you sense that you are acquainting yourself with a place of great achievement and splendor. You feel more and more what a great privilege it will be if you are employed there. If you have any integrity in your soul, you will also make a firm commitment that if you are ever finally called into employment, you will want to give your best to uphold the values associated with this institution.

Jesus is gloriously magnificent. He is a person of absolute excellence. He is on the opposite end of the scale compared to what this sin-sick world offers. Ten thousand times ten thousand angels attend His throne and worship Him. He has called you to Himself and into His kingdom. You cannot simply walk into His kingdom with a casual attitude as if you were walking into your own bedroom. You cannot live in His kingdom with shallow spirituality and worldly carnality. That is an absolute contradiction. You ought to be aiming for the same glory and excellence of life that He has. As you consider who He is, you sense that there are heights of spirituality and godliness that you need to rise to. Thankfully, Peter tells us that the power of Jesus provides you with everything you need to rise to those heights. As you know Him more and more, His power works in you to will and to do His good pleasure.

Pastors' children suffer because of this, often unfairly. When anyone finds out that they have been misbehaving, they chide them saying, "How can you do this? You are a pastor's child. You ought to be ashamed of yourself." The logic is that because the child comes from a home that is dignified with spirituality, he or she should also live an exemplary life of godliness. I say it is often unfair because children should be given space to be childish. It is part of the joy of childhood. Also, the unconverted cannot be expected to live like the converted. They ought to be urged to become Christians rather than to conform to an inward life that is totally foreign to them. All the same, society expects them to live in conformity to their parents' calling. Whereas this is unfair for the pastor's unconverted little children, it is not unfair for those whom Jesus Christ calls into His kingdom. This is because His divine power enables us to pursue a life that shows something of His glory and excellence.

Through His Promises Granted to Us

Within the "all things" given to us for our growth, we have God's own promises. The apostle Peter writes, "By which have been given to us exceedingly great and precious promises, that through these you may be partakers of the divine nature, having escaped the corruption that is in the world through lust" (2 Peter 1:4). That is quite a mouthful. Let us break that down into smaller pieces that are easier to swallow.

It is worth noting that Christianity is about responding to the promises of God in faith. It is about trusting a God who is faithful to His promises. The Christian begins their spiritual life with promises such as, "Whoever calls on the name of the LORD shall be saved" (Rom. 10:13) and "Come to Me, all you who labor and are heavy laden, and I will give you rest" (Matt. 11:28). The sinner under conviction of sin calls on the name of the Lord and comes to Christ for salvation based on such promises. He believes God and thus is saved.

In my evangelistic work, people ask me how they will know if God will truly answer their cry for salvation. My answer is that God Himself will assure them. He will do what He has promised. They should concentrate on their response: they should come to Him in repentance and faith. As the apostle John puts it, "If we confess our sins, He is faithful and just to forgive us our sins and to cleanse us from all unrighteousness" (1 John 1:9). Our God is a faithful God. He not only gives us promises but also keeps His word. He will always fulfill what He promises.

The precious and very great promises of God go beyond those related to our salvation. Many more buoy us through the storms of life as we make our way to heaven. Others are in our armory as we fight the good fight of the faith. This is why they are so precious and very great. These promises are scattered all over the Scriptures. The apostle Peter does not quote any promises here. He simply informs his readers about the fruit of those promises. He says that "through these you may be partakers of the divine nature." We noted earlier that Jesus is all-glorious and excellent. The blinding splendor of His holiness shines brighter than the sun at noonday. He has given us His great and glorious promises so that we can experience ever-increasing life as we journey toward heaven. As we trust in these promises we not only win many battles along our way to glory but also grow to become more like Christ.

We rest on the promises of God for our salvation. We must also rest on the promises of God for our sanctification. Just as we cried to be delivered and pardoned from our sin when we first came to Christ, we must continue crying out for this deliverance in our lives as believers. God will faithfully continue to sanctify us more and more each time we come to Him in repentance and faith as His children. It does not matter what sins we are struggling with. We must continue to make use of these great and precious promises of God as His children. They are all ours!

There is no excuse for a believer to give up fighting sin; in light of God's promises, sin should not have mastery over His children. God doesn't want us to become content with making our journey to heaven in "economy class." He wants all of us to be upgrading as we grow in our Christian lives. Through His promises, He will faithfully upgrade you as you work out your salvation with fear and trembling. Is there some sin in your life that is robbing you of peace with God? Take it to Him in prayer and plead His promises. Like David in the Old Testament, pray to Him, saying, "Purge me with hyssop, and I shall be clean; wash me, and I shall be whiter than snow.... Restore to me the joy of Your salvation, and uphold me by Your generous Spirit" (Ps. 51:7, 12). He will do it because He has promised to do so. He is a faithful God.

I love the way the apostle Peter refers to our sanctification as "[becoming] partakers of the divine nature, having escaped the corruption that is in the world through lust." The word *partake* is the famous Greek word for fellowship—*koinonia*. Peter is not simply referring to believers manifesting greater godliness; he is also implying the notion of having fellowship with God in His holy nature. Interacting with God in spiritual fellowship is how we grow as Christians. It is similar to how an ordinary piece of iron can be turned into a magnet. You simply rub it against a magnet several times. Before long, its atoms line up in the same way as the magnet and it becomes magnetic as well. We, too, share in God's nature through this life lived with Him, having escaped from the world's corruption.

If there is anything we have learned from these two verses in 2 Peter 1, it is the fact that we have no excuse not to live a truly godly life. Our triune God—Father, Son, and Holy Spirit—has provided everything we need to live such a life. Everything. Just as I have that full-body gym equipment in my home, we all have what we need to reach optimum spiritual health and growth. We must be very concerned when someone who claims to have been a Christian for several years still exhibits the struggles of a young believer. We should challenge such a person to examine whether they are truly in the faith. We must be deliberate about our spiritual growth. People should not take comfort in the fact that they said some prayer a few years ago or that they signed a decision card. Spiritual life should show itself by a vibrant faith lived in fellowship with God as we grow to be more like Him.

I have no doubt that one reason for this lackluster Christian life abounding all around us is that Christians are content with a lack of spiritual knowledge. Remember, we noted that spiritual growth is "through the knowledge of Him who called us." We live in an age of information overload. We are bombarded with information and news literally every second through television and the Internet. Our mobile devices are always with us and are constantly beeping for our attention. As a result, we are spending less and less time listening to good preaching and reading the Bible and other Christian books that can build us up. Our minds are being filled with the world's garbage, and as a result our lives are spewing out the same filth. Our minds are famished of heavenly information that truly nourishes the soul. We need to pursue greater self-discipline in deliberately carving out time to feed the mind with the bread of heaven so that we may truly grow as believers. "As newborn babes, desire the pure milk of the word, that you may grow thereby" (1 Peter 2:2). This cannot be overemphasized. It is only when we do this that we will start seeing more Christians exhibiting maturity and Christlikeness.

I cannot think of a better way to end this chapter than to quote the hymn "How Firm a Foundation," composed by an anonymous hymn writer from the eighteenth century. It describes some of the precious and very great promises that God has given us in Christ.

> How firm a foundation, you saints of the Lord,
> Is laid for your faith in his excellent Word!
> What more can he say than to you he has said,
> To you who for refuge to Jesus have fled?
>
> Fear not, I am with you, O be not dismayed;
> For I am your God, and will still give you aid;
> I'll strengthen you, help you, and cause you to stand,
> Upheld by my righteous, omnipotent hand.
>
> When through the deep waters I call you to go,
> The rivers of sorrow shall not overflow;
> For I will be with you, your troubles to bless,
> And sanctify to you your deepest distress.
>
> When through fiery trials your pathway shall lie,
> My grace, all-sufficient, shall be your supply;
> The flame shall not hurt you; I only design
> Your dross to consume and your gold to refine.
>
> E'en down to old age all my people shall prove
> My sovereign, eternal, unchangeable love;

And when hoary hairs shall their temples adorn,
Like lambs they shall still in my bosom be borne.

The soul that on Jesus has leaned for repose,
I will not, I will not desert to his foes;
That soul, though all hell should endeavor to shake,
I'll never, no never, no never forsake.[1]

---

1. "How Firm a Foundation," Hymnary.org, accessed February 2, 2024, https://hymnary.org/hymn/TH1990/94.

PART 2

The Imperatives of Spiritual Growth

CHAPTER 3

Make Every Effort to Grow Up

For this very reason, giving all diligence, add to your faith virtue, to virtue knowledge.

—2 PETER 1:5

Once a year, I pay my annual insurance bill, and after that I don't think about it for the next twelve months. I know that if anything goes wrong in the days ahead, I am covered. My mind is at peace. Nothing more is required apart from that financial transaction that takes place every year. Sadly, many believers treat the Christian faith that way—like some kind of hellfire insurance policy. They transacted with Jesus Christ on the day of their salvation and now they are at peace. If they die, they will go to heaven. Between now and then, they can simply get on with their lives like anyone else. Of course, they must go to church on a weekly basis and keep away from obvious outward sins like violence, sexual immorality, stealing, and telling lies. Beyond that, there is really nothing more to their Christian lives.

That is not the picture the Bible paints. According to Scripture, the Christian life is much more than something you secure in one moment to make sure you escape hell. It is a life you grow up in. You mature with time. You make progress, and as you make that progress, the Lord uses you as a means of blessing His church and the world. You become more and more effective and fruitful. Yet this picture of maturity is not the most common picture of believers today. Rather, many are content simply to go to church and then move on to worldly activities if they are not considered harmful to one's spiritual life. I fear that many professing believers will arrive on the other side of death with very little to show for the lives they lived on earth. Jesus will not say to them, "I was hungry and you gave Me food; I was thirsty and you gave Me drink; I was a stranger and you took Me in; I was naked and you clothed Me; I was sick and you visited Me; I was in prison and you came to Me…. Assuredly, I say to you, inasmuch as you did it to one of the least of these My brethren, you did it to Me" (Matt. 25:35–36, 40). God has saved you so that He may use you here on earth. He will use you more and more as you mature and grow in your Christian life.

Thus far, we have observed several indicatives from 2 Peter 1. First, we're told that we have a "like precious faith" with all other believers (v. 1). Second, we've seen that God has given to us all things that we need for life and godliness through His own power (v. 3). Third, we saw that through this power, God has given us His great and precious promises (v. 4). Through these promises we are made partakers of the divine nature and are helped to escape the corruption that is in the world. All these are true of each one of us if we are genuine believers in the Lord Jesus Christ.

This is the basis of what Peter goes on to say in verse 5: "For this very reason, giving all diligence, add to your faith virtue." This is the logical consequence of the three indicatives that Peter mentioned in the earlier verses. We must make every effort to grow up.

The Christian Faith Is Reasonable

The Christian faith uses the brain because the brain is God's gift to you. As a result, it is sensible and rational. In the Christian faith you are expected to think logically. You should learn to extrapolate. Say to yourself, "If this is true and this is true, then this also ought to be true." That is the Christian faith. It demands that we should be a thinking people who are intelligent enough to appreciate what the Lord has done for us and the consequences that follow from that truth. If He has died for us, how then should we live for Him? It is simple logic that you should process on your own.

Let me use two examples to illustrate this point. If you are a married man, you will know that when you were a bachelor, you did whatever you wanted to do without consulting anyone. You would spend most of your evenings hanging out with your friends. You returned home at any time you wanted. Then a time came when you married your wife. Did your social life have to change? Of course it did! You could not simply call home from the office and tell your wife, "Hey, honey, I will be hanging out with the guys this evening. See you whenever we are done." If you attempted that, you know your wife would remind you in no uncertain terms that you are now a married man and need to behave like one. Those old habits need to change. You cannot continue coming home in the early hours of the morning. Your wife left her home, her friends, and her family to come and live with you as husband and wife. A lot changed in her life. A lot had better change in yours too. If God has also blessed your marriage with children, then the extrapolation goes even further. You need to plan your day and budget your finances with those children in mind. You must now pour your life into their holistic development. You must feed, clothe, and educate those children. They are your responsibility. You cannot continue with life as if you were still a bachelor. It only makes sense. You need to say to yourself, "Since I am now a husband and a father, it is only logical that I rise to the challenge of marriage and family life."

We can say the same about our responsibilities toward our parents. You were once a child. Your parents poured their all into bringing you up and making you what you are now. You are educated and have a job, while they are now retired and battling with the consequences of encroaching old age. You did not fall from the sky like the famous British comedic character Mr. Bean. Your mother gave birth to you. You were blessed through your parents' tireless efforts while they still had strength. It only makes sense that you do not look the other way now that you have grown up and they are in need. You should support them in their old age. Christianity is like that. It is reasonable. The blessings of God that have been laid out by the apostle Peter in the first verses of this chapter demand a logical response from you as a Christian.

The apostle Paul often argued this way too. He begins Romans 12 by stating, "I beseech you therefore, brethren, by the mercies of God, that you present your bodies a living sacrifice, holy, acceptable to God, which is your reasonable service" (v. 1). He is saying that "in view of God's mercy" (as the NIV renders this verse), it only makes sense that Christians should give their all to God. The blessing of God is indescribable; therefore, our response should also be equally extraordinary. The apostle Paul earlier tried to capture something of his own amazement at the superabundant grace of God when he wrote, "Oh, the depth of the riches both of the wisdom and knowledge of God! How unsearchable are His judgments and His ways past finding out! 'For who has known the mind of the LORD? Or who has become His counselor?' 'Or who has first given to Him and it shall be repaid to him?' For of Him and through Him and to Him are all things, to whom be glory forever. Amen" (Rom. 11:33–36). In light of all this, Christians should surrender themselves as living sacrifices to God.

That is what Peter is saying in our text. God has given us the same faith that He gave to our spiritual heroes. He has also given us His own power to enable us to live a spiritual and godly life. He has added to this the blessing of His great and glorious promises. There must be a logical response to this. You cannot go on living with a lackluster attitude toward God. That would not make sense.

You Must Make an Effort to Grow

The logical response that we make to the superabundant grace of God in our lives should not be a mere knee-jerk reaction. It needs to go beyond the initial joy of conversion. It must be a hearty diligence that remains consistent to the very end of our lives on earth.

Our English translation reads, "Giving all diligence, add to your faith virtue," but there is a Greek word that is not captured here, simply because it is difficult to put it into proper English sentence construction. It is the word *pareisenengkantes*, which means "bringing in alongside of." The actual sentence should read something like, "Bring alongside every effort to supply to your faith." D. Edmond Hiebert in his commentary on 2 Peter suggests that this is an effort you make alongside what God is doing in your life. God has given you His gift of faith, His power, and His glorious promises. Bring alongside these divine blessings every effort of your own by adding virtue to this God-given faith.

This is the nature of the Christian life. In initial salvation, God acts alone. We do not cooperate with Him, because we are spiritually dead. We simply respond when He infuses spiritual life into us. Our response is in terms of repentance and faith. However, in sanctification, we cooperate with Him. He is active in our lives, and so are we. He convicts us when we do wrong. He inspires us. He leads us. He guides us. There is so much that God does in our lives. But you grow when you supplement that with your active cooperation. You do something alongside what God is doing. In other words, sanctification is a joint effort.

The apostle Peter says that you must eagerly bring in your own effort to ensure your spiritual growth. You must show urgency. There is a difference between the way you groom in the morning during the week (especially when you wake up late) and the way you do so over the weekend. On a weekday, you hurriedly jump into the shower while still brushing your teeth, throw on some clothes, put together a quick breakfast, and zoom past everyone in the house as you head out the front door into the car. You are in a hurry, and everyone around you can see that. Over the weekend, you turn in your bed like a door on its hinge. There is some movement, but you do not go anywhere. The apostle Peter is saying we must be in haste. The energy you invest goes a long way in showing that you are on to something that is worth the effort—your spiritual growth. You are not on holiday. You are working out your salvation "with fear and trembling," to borrow the words of the apostle Paul (Phil. 2:12).

To make this even more demanding, Peter adds in the word *all*. He says you should give all diligence. In other words, you must spare nothing in seeking to achieve this. You must never be half-hearted in this task. It is the way an individual who is preparing for a major athletic competition goes into training. If they know that they need to bring down their weight by ten pounds to qualify in their class for the competition, you can be sure they will do whatever is necessary to lose weight. They will not spare any effort whatsoever to achieve that goal. If they know that they need to achieve a particular speed to win the race, they will set aside time daily to ensure that they beat that time. Their coach will be there with a stopwatch tracking their progress. They know they will need to do resistance exercises and spend regular time in the gym to tone their muscles. They will not simply do what they feel like doing. They have a goal—to win that medal—and so they will spare no effort to achieve that. If it means also taking supplements, they will take them religiously. If they need to be sleeping eight hours per day, they will ensure they do that as well. Winning a race is not about chance. It is about discipline and goal setting. It is about sparing nothing to achieve all.

That is how you should view the Christian life and your spiritual growth. God has given you faith, His power, and His great promises. How are you responding to all this? Sadly, many believers are characterized by chronic laziness. Their lives show no signs of earnestness to attain any spiritual goals. They think that spiritual growth just happens. There is no processing of any logical deduction. That needs to change if today's Christians will impact our generation to the glory of God.

You Must Diligently Add to Your Faith

Christian growth is about increasing in Christian graces. The apostle Peter says, "For this very reason, giving all diligence, add to your faith virtue, to virtue knowledge, to knowledge self-control, to self-control perseverance, to perseverance godliness, to godliness brotherly kindness, and to brotherly kindness love" (2 Peter 1:5–7). We often see the word *add* used when a donor gives you something that you need to achieve a goal. The Greek word indicates a generous provision. If you are going to build a state-of-the-art university campus, you will not begrudge anyone who gives you whatever they can afford, even if it is one dollar. However, you will be praying for a rich benefactor who will generously donate millions of dollars. That is the only way that such a university campus can be built. Peter is urging believers to do that for their own spiritual growth. They should add generous portions of the spiritual qualities he mentions to their lives. That is how maturity is achieved and sustained in the Christian life.

A scene in the Christian movie *Fireproof* perfectly illustrates this principle. Caleb and Catherine Holt's marriage was falling apart. Caleb's father urged him not to give up on his marriage and gave him a book that laid out forty steps he needed to take—one step per day—to salvage his marriage. Initially, Caleb followed those instructions half-heartedly, out of a sense of duty to his father and not out of love for his wife. On one of those days, he was supposed to order a bouquet of flowers. He called up a supplier who gave him various options, with the best bouquet being the most expensive. He settled for one of the cheapest ones. Of course, when his wife returned home and saw the flowers, she was not impressed with them. The absence of love resulted in the absence of generosity. His wife could not be fooled. If you truly love your wife, you go the extra mile. You will want to give her a bountiful supply.

While we may laugh at Caleb's pathetic attempt to convince his wife not to divorce him by purchasing cheap flowers for her, is this not what we are often guilty of with respect to our relationship with God? We give minimal attention to the things of God but somehow expect great fruit from it. Look, for instance, at how much time you give to reading your Bible and Christian books. Compare that to the time you spend in recreational activities like watching sports on television. Which one gets a generous portion of your time? This can also be applied to our commitment to Christian fellowship and other means of grace. We want spiritual growth at the cheapest cost. God has given us everything, but we want to give Him next to nothing. That is certainly not logical. We must come alongside God with a generous portion of our effort.

God has formed the lives of believers on a strong, sturdy foundation. The question is, What are you now using to build on the superstructure of your spiritual life? If, on one hand, you use mud, poles, and grass, then you should not be surprised if your life does not withstand the storms of life. No one dares to take shelter in your miserly life. If, on the other hand, you use sturdy materials of the best quality, then your generosity will pay off.

Imagine two individuals who become Christians at the same time. If you fast-forward twenty years, you find that perhaps one of them simply goes to church but hardly bears any fruit, while the other one may be a leader in the church. The first one may have messed up his life due to unwise and unspiritual decisions made along the way, while the second one may be busy discipling many others in what it means to be a follower of Jesus Christ in this world. What makes the difference between these two individuals? It is not the initial foundation laid by God. It is often the spiritual lethargy that is present in a person's life. Laziness is costly. Each one of us has a foundation that can produce a true spiritual giant. If we can only do what this verse is telling us to do—make every effort to grow up—we would in due season build a spiritual life that would impact the world for Christ.

We must echo the words of Johnson Oatman Jr. (1856–1922) in his hymn "Higher Ground":

> I'm pressing on the upward way,
> New heights I'm gaining ev'ry day;
> Still praying as I'm onward bound,
> "Lord, plant my feet on higher ground."

Lord, lift me up, and let me stand
By faith, on heaven's tableland;
A higher plane than I have found,
Lord, plant my feet on higher ground.[1]

---

1. Johnson Oatman Jr., "Higher Ground," Hymnary.org, accessed February 2, 2024, https://hymnary.org/text/im_pressing_on_the_upward_way.

CHAPTER 4

Strive for Excellence

Giving all diligence, add to your faith virtue.
—2 PETER 1:5

Every church should be committed to growth. This growth should be quantitative, yes, but also qualitative. It should delight the souls of God's people to see new converts baptized and added to the church. It should also please God's people to see those who were struggling initially now being effective and fruitful in their Christian walk. Every church should long to grow in depth as well as width. Every church leader should ask, "Are God's people in this church growing in grace?" This is what the apostle Peter was longing to see among the believers in the dispersion.

We have thus far seen how the apostle has written about the foundational realities that are already true of every believer. He has written about all of us having a faith of equal standing with all other believers, the divine power through which we are granted all things necessary for life and godliness, and God's precious and very great promises by which we participate in His divine nature as we escape from the corruption of the world. These are the indicatives we must not lose sight of.

In the last chapter, we noted how the apostle Peter changed gears and started giving imperatives with the words "giving all diligence, add…" This is our duty. We are to purposefully bring certain qualities into our lives alongside the faith we already have. It is by making this effort that we begin to experience spiritual growth. Peter breaks down the areas in which this growth must manifest itself. It is tempting to think that since he only briefly mentions each of these areas, we should also quickly pass over them and move on to the implications of spiritual growth. However, if we do this, we will fail to see the very reason why Peter takes time to list each of these qualities. They are strokes made on the canvas by a master artist who is painting a portrait of what a mature Christian ought to look like. With each stroke, we should be asking ourselves, Am I deliberately ensuring that this quality is part of my life in an ever-increasing way? In the next few chapters we will look at each of these areas in more detail.

A Working Definition of *Virtue*

Peter writes, "Giving all diligence, add to your faith virtue." Our first task is to understand what he means by the word *virtue*, or *excellence* as some translations have it. He already used this term in verse 3 when he wrote, "His divine power has given to us all things that pertain to life and godliness, through the knowledge of Him who called us by glory and virtue." So, what does virtue mean?

I would say virtue or excellence means that something achieves its intended purpose to the highest degree possible. For instance, when you say that someone is an excellent student, you mean that the person is never content with average grades but gives himself to mastering the subject matter. He is very attentive during classes, does a great job in researching when doing his assignments, gives attention to details when composing his written work, and ensures that he beats the deadline for submission. When such a student is in your class, you can say you have an excellent student. Similarly, if a manager refers to a subordinate as an excellent worker, it means the person hardly ever needs supervision. He reports for work on time, does a solid job on any task he is given, and suggests ways of improving productivity. The supervisor or manager can afford to pay attention to other matters. He knows that with such an employee under his supervision, he does not need to worry. What about an excellent car? It not only gets you to your destination but is good on fuel consumption and very comfortable. It is strong, durable, and reliable. Even the music system is out of this world. In other words, it has exceeded your expectations. It is just…excellent!

Many illustrations of virtue are given in the Bible. There is the virtuous or excellent wife of Proverbs 31. I will let the author explain how a lady achieves her role as a woman, a wife, and a mother with excellence:

> Who can find a virtuous wife? For her worth is far above rubies. The heart of her husband safely trusts her; so he will have no lack of gain. She does him good and not evil all the days of her life. She seeks wool and flax, and willingly works with her hands. She is like the merchant ships, she brings her food from afar. She also rises while it is yet night, and provides food for her household, and a portion for her maidservants. She considers a field and buys it; from her profits she plants a vineyard. She girds herself with strength, and strengthens her arms. She perceives that her merchandise is good, and her lamp does not go out by night. She stretches out her hands to the distaff, and her hand holds the spindle. She extends her hand to the poor, yes, she reaches out her hands to the needy. She is not afraid of snow for her household, for all her household is clothed with scarlet. She makes tapestry for herself; her clothing is fine linen and purple. Her husband is known in the gates, when he sits among the elders of the land. She makes linen garments and sells them, and supplies sashes for the merchants. Strength and honor are her clothing; she shall rejoice in time to come. She opens her mouth with wisdom, and on her tongue is the law of kindness. She watches over the ways of her household, and does not eat the bread of idleness. Her children rise up and call her blessed; her husband also, and he praises her: "Many daughters have done well, but you excel them all." Charm is deceitful and beauty is passing, but a woman who fears the LORD, she shall be praised. Give her of the fruit of her hands, and let her own works praise her in the gates. (Prov. 31:10–31)

This almost takes your breath away! Yet that is often what happens when we observe excellence and virtue.

Virtue Applied to the Other Qualities

One aspect of virtue that can easily be missed is the energy exerted to achieve this excellence. In each of the examples we have looked at— the student, the worker, the car, and the wife of Proverbs 31—energy is being expended to produce brilliant fruit. We must not miss that. Peter is emphasizing that we must never content ourselves with a lethargic, half-hearted, mediocre Christian life. You must build the superstructure of a strong moral life with God's help, and it must be done with excellence and virtue. This is what He has called you to. You are to exert your utmost energy to achieve moral distinction in your spiritual life. Let us apply this to the remaining six qualities that make up these imperatives. Each will be explained separately in the coming chapters. For now all I want us to see is that this all-round attitude of virtue or excellence must characterize each one.

Knowledge

There must be virtue in your pursuit and attainment of the knowledge of God and His ways. Unlike most believers who approach Bible study lethargically or simply assume they have adequate knowledge, you should be like the first-century believers of whom it was said, "They continued steadfastly in the apostles' doctrine" (Acts 2:42). You should be like the excellent student we considered earlier. You should never have the attitude that any Christian doctrine is for others to understand—like the pastor or church elders or ministry leaders—but not for you. You should want to be the best that you possibly can be in terms of your knowledge of spiritual truths, even if you have never been to Bible college.

Self-Control

Temptations will never come to an end while you are on earth. Yet you are expected to defeat sin more and more as you grow in your

Christian life. To do this, there must be a growing excellence in your pursuit and attainment of self-control. You should say no not only to the world and the devil but also to yourself. With the help of the Holy Spirit, you should gain the highest possible hold of yourself in all areas of your inner life, such as your temper (anger), your sexual urges (lust), your desire to acquire whatever others have (envy), your tendency toward laziness (slothfulness), your appetite for food (gluttony), and your sense of self-importance (pride).

Steadfastness

The Christian life is not like a hundred-meter sprint. It is like a marathon. You should stay the course with consistent stamina. The Bible says, "The path of the just is like the shining sun, that shines ever brighter unto the perfect day" (Prov. 4:18). This speaks of the steadfast growth that must characterize true believers. You should aim for a life that distinctly shows this quality. There is no use speaking about self-control if it lasts only a short while before you return to your spiritual vomit. Your loyalty to Christ and His kingdom should be unwavering, whatever tests and temptations come your way. This is what makes you dependable in the church. Your commitment needs to be of the highest order.

Godliness

I hope to show you, when we look at this quality in more detail later, that godliness is the apex of the qualities that Peter speaks about here. To be godly is simply to be godlike in terms of moral and spiritual qualities. It means being devout and holy. It means being authentically religious and heavenly minded. Your knowledge, self-control, and steadfastness should well up into a godliness like that of Job in the Old Testament of whom God boasted, saying, "Have you considered My servant Job, that there is none like him on the earth, a blameless and upright man, one who fears God and shuns evil?" (Job 1:8). Being virtuous in godliness is to passionately want to be like God in everything.

Brotherly Kindness

A person pursuing true godliness will be touched by the needs and sufferings of others who are also children of God. The overflow of this godliness will result in acts of mercy toward their brethren. This is why the quality of brotherly kindness follows that of godliness. Peter is urging believers to personally ensure that they do not hold back when it comes to expressing affection within the household of faith. If we think of the heart like a tap, it should be turned all the way open and allowed to gush out its refreshing contents onto God's people. It is to such that Jesus will say on judgment day, "Assuredly, I say to you, inasmuch as you did it to one of the least of these My brethren, you did it to Me" (Matt. 25:40).

Love

The heart that loves the people of God in truth will also love all other human beings because they, too, are made in the image of God—as marred as that image might be. Love is costly because it is more than mere sentimentality. It involves giving—giving time, giving attention, giving money and property, giving food. It may also involve giving your life. Since godliness is being like God, this is the highest mark we can aim at, because God is love (1 John 4:8, 16). Indeed, "For God so loved the world that He gave His only begotten Son" (John 3:16). God loved a fallen, sinful, and rebellious world so much that He gave His own Son in exchange. This is the excellence of love to which we are being called!

Virtue Applied to Life in General

Virtue and excellence should be realized in all the qualities we pursue in the quest for growth. It should also be seen in our various spheres of life as believers. We saw it in the example of the virtuous wife of Proverbs 31. Her primary area of influence was in domestic life. She ensured that every part of it received her utmost attention. Her husband and children were well taken care of, and she was good at buying and selling at a profit. She ensured her family was well fed and clothed. She grew things not only for food but also for selling. She also expressed love to those who were needy by supplying them with what they lacked as much as it was in her power to do so. She taught her children the ways of wisdom and the ways of God. She ensured that her home was aesthetically beautiful. The list goes on. She invested the necessary energy in her sphere of responsibility and, as a result, excellence was written all over her life.

We have seen that faith is the foundation on which we continue to build the superstructure of our lives. People do not see your faith itself, because faith is internal. What they see is the life you live. Peter is telling you to let others see your virtue. Let them see moral distinction. Exert yourself to the utmost so that all this can be seen in you. Instead of merely admiring the woman in Proverbs 31, imitate her in your own life and areas of influence. Are you a husband? You have an even greater challenge. The apostle Paul says, "Husbands, love your wives, just as Christ also loved the church and gave Himself for her" (Eph. 5:25). That is the level of excellence to which you are called. Be deliberate about seeking to attain this. Live in such a way that your daughters will want to marry a man like you and your sons will want to emulate your example when they marry. Die in such a way that your wife and children will look at your grave and say, "Here lies a man who showed us what it meant to love one's family. We could not have wished for a better husband and father. He exemplified true godliness."

Perhaps you are still a young person in the home but are already converted to Christ. You, too, should aim for excellence as an expression of your faith in the Lord Jesus Christ. Your parents should see the highest levels of responsibility and obedience to their parental oversight. They should consider you trustworthy and hardworking at home, doing your chores with little or no supervision. You should be seeking to obey them as you seek to obey Christ. That should be the expression of your faith. Your parents should be able to testify that they have seen this manifesting itself in you increasingly since you made your profession of faith in the Lord Jesus Christ.

Let us apply this to the workplace, where you spend the better part of your weekday. Even there, you should seek to supplement your faith with virtue. You should work as unto the Lord and not merely to earn your salary. You should "be obedient to those who are your masters according to the flesh, with fear and trembling, in sincerity of heart, as to Christ; not with eyeservice, as men-pleasers, but as bondservants of Christ, doing the will of God from the heart, with goodwill doing service, as to the Lord, and not to men" (Eph. 6:5–7). You should aim to show moral and spiritual distinction in an ever-growing way that expresses itself in genuine hard work and trustworthiness in your workplace.

Finally, let us apply this to church life. You should aim for a quality of church life that shows you truly treasure the church as the glorious bride of Christ. Virtue in this respect means you are a church member your leaders can depend on. You will have carved out time in your busy life for church meetings and activities so that they are not crowded out by any other business in your life. You should aim to genuinely love your brothers and sisters in Christ in the local church, ensuring that you are ever covering them with your prayers and are available when they need a shoulder to cry on. This love includes being long-suffering and patient with others in the church when they are constantly rubbing you the wrong way. Excellence here also expresses itself in the way you use your time, gifts, and finances to support the ministries of the church—including its work of missions.

Virtue Is Not the Same as Perfection

Let us be clear. We are not talking about perfection here. Rather, making every effort to supplement your faith with virtue refers to something you should be working toward with all your ransomed powers. You should be a believer who is characterized by ener-getically pursuing moral distinction. Only our Lord Jesus Christ is perfect. Our task is to become more and more like Him. We do so by pouring all our energies into this pursuit. We fail to make progress in that direction because we are too laid-back about spiritual things. Thus, people do not see our lives as a shining example of virtue in contrast to the non-Christians around us. There is hardly any difference, except the fact that we go to church on Sunday as a regular habit and they do not. They hear us engaged in as much gossip and slander as they are. They notice that at the first excuse, we gladly miss church. They notice that we dress to show off as much as they do. They see that we try to get away with as little work as possible in the workplace—just the way they do. All this is often because we do not make a conscious effort to add spiritual excellence to our Christian walk. We allow ourselves to be mediocre as long as we do not fall into the worst form of scandalous sins. Again, this is not about perfection but rather seeking to reach the highest levels of godliness in all areas of our lives to God's glory.

Let me end by stating that supplementing your faith with virtue comes with a lot of deliberate self-discipline and practice. Excellence is a product of resolve and exercise. A few years ago, one of the most well-known soccer players in England was David Beckham. He was particularly famous for the way he used to bend the trajectory of a ball when he kicked it toward the goal. As you can well imagine, he was very good with his free kicks. From a spot on the ground, he would kick the ball in one direction and then in midair it would curve and enter the corner of a goalpost with surgical precision. He often scored because the goalkeeper would judge the direction of the ball by its initial direction. By the time the goalie realized the ball was in fact heading into the goal, it was often too late for him to do anything. This gave birth to the phrase "Bend it like Beckham." On one occasion, I watched a video of his training sessions and realized that apart from his exceptional gifts, he spent hours upon hours perfecting the art of kicking the ball the way he did. He spent mountains of time and effort and energy alone with a ball on the pitch, trying again and again. The result of the resolve and the constant practice was that he got better and better. His performance on the soccer pitch in front of tens of thousands of fans was the fruit of what he had been doing when he was practicing alone and sometimes with teammates. He exerted his utmost energy into achieving the distinction that he became well known for. That is how we are to supplement our faith with virtue. Mere wishful thinking will not do it. We must give all our diligence to achieve this.

The apostle Paul held this same attitude about the spiritual life. Writing to the Corinthians, he said, "Do you not know that those who run in a race all run, but one receives the prize? Run in such a way that you may obtain it. And everyone who competes for the prize is temperate in all things. Now they do it to obtain a perishable crown, but we for an imperishable crown. Therefore I run thus: not with uncertainty. Thus I fight: not as one who beats the air. But I discipline my body and bring it into subjection, lest, when I have preached to others, I myself should become disqualified" (1 Cor. 9:24–27). He exerts himself, making every effort to be a self-disciplined person. That is the attitude we all should have toward our spiritual lives.

If you are not interested in doing this, then most likely it is because you are not a Christian. You are merely religious. You may be a member of a church, but if you are not interested in exhibiting that moral energy to become more and more like Jesus, then most likely you have never been made a true Christian. If you die the way you are now, you will go to hell despite being a church member. I said at the beginning that we must be deliberate about our spiritual growth. If you are content with a closed Bible, an empty prayer closet, and casual church attendance, then you are still spiritually dead.

The Christian life is a race. Nobody who competes in a race is content with coming in second. All runners put in great effort. They may not be the winners in the end, but you can still see that they put in everything they could to win the race. That is why we should be concerned about those who are on the church membership roll but never strike a blow for Jesus. They are merely content to be there and to speak about a day many years ago when they gave their life to Jesus. Such a life is a back door into hell. If this describes you, the biggest favor you can do for yourself is to go to Christ and say to

Him, *Savior, save me in such a way that there will be genuine godly energy, real desire, and hunger for godliness within me. Let there be true godliness in all spheres of my life, a godliness that shines. Let there be a godliness that is so distinct from the world that people will notice that You've saved me. Jesus, please save me.*

None of us will ever arrive at the height of godliness that Jesus had while He walked this earth. Even the woman in Proverbs 31 would have told you that she had woes. She had desires that were not satisfied. She had unaccomplished tasks and things she was still praying about with respect to her own family and her businesses. Only Jesus has arrived. If you are a genuine believer, then you will always be striving to add virtue to your faith. You will be praying for more godliness. When you go into your closet, your chief prayer request will not be for a new car, a new job, or a new dress; it will be for more godliness. Your prayer will be,

> Take my life and let it be
> Consecrated, Lord, to thee.
> Take my moments and my days;
> Let them flow in endless praise,
> Let them flow in endless praise.
>
> Take my love; my Lord, I pour
> At thy feet its treasures store.
> Take myself, and I will be
> Ever, only, all for thee,
> Ever, only, all for thee.[1]

That becomes your utmost prayer because that is what you really want. That is true Christianity.

---

1. Frances R. Havergal, "Take My Life, and Let It Be," Hymnary.org, accessed February 2, 2024, https://hymnary.org/text/take_my_life_and_let_it_be.

CHAPTER 5

Deepen Your Knowledge

Giving all diligence, add…to virtue knowledge.
— 2 PETER 1:5

Every believer is meant to be on an upward spiritual trajectory, a trajectory of growth. The apostle Peter can say this because of what God has already done to secure this growth in each one of His children. This is evident in the indicatives of 2 Peter 1:1–4.

Beginning in verse 5, Peter tells us of the areas in which we must be responsible for our own growth. We must be energetic as we build our spiritual lives on top of this substructure that God has put in place. We must build on it by adding virtue, knowledge, and so on. It is only as we do so that our lives can grow to become skyscrapers for the glory of God. We must not be indolent but must put all our energies into ensuring that all areas of our spiritual lives speak of excellence.

In this chapter, we will discuss the second imperative that we are to add to our faith—knowledge. The apostle Peter says, "Giving all diligence, add to your faith virtue, to virtue knowledge." This flies in the face of the saying, "Ignorance is the mother of devotion." This insinuates that if you know too much about Christian doctrine, it deprives you of commitment to God. It propagates the view that in order to be overflowing with zeal, you must not think too much. What matters is that your heart is full of feelings of love for God. That is not biblical. That is not the way God intended Christianity to be. Rather, our faith must be informed, and our virtue needs to be intelligent. We need an excellence in knowledge and a knowledge-able excellence.

What Is This Knowledge?

The Bible speaks about a spiritual ignorance that characterizes unbe-lievers. That basic ignorance is what causes them to live as creatures of instinct, morally speaking. The apostle Peter spoke about this in his first epistle: "Therefore gird up the loins of your mind, be sober, and rest your hope fully upon the grace that is to be brought to you at the revelation of Jesus Christ; as obedient children, not conforming your-selves to the former lusts, as in your ignorance; but as He who called you is holy, you also be holy in all your conduct" (1 Peter 1:13–15). In speaking about "the former lusts, as in your ignorance," Peter is teaching us that there was a time before our conversion when we did not know about God and holy things. To be sure, we had some vague intellectual knowledge, but that was woefully insufficient to enable us to live a holy life. Instead, our lives were conformed to our fallen instincts and passions. The very process of becoming Christians involved a gaining of knowledge. We heard about the fact that God demanded a righteousness and holiness that we did not have and could never hope to produce. We learned about Jesus, who lived and died for us to procure for us this righteousness and holiness. By the help of the Holy Spirit, we believed this teaching and embraced Jesus Christ as our Savior. The more we heard and understood all this, the more we came to this solid assurance of our personal salvation in Christ. So, becoming a Christian involves gaining knowledge—the knowledge of the gospel.

When Peter says that we should add knowledge to virtue, part of that knowledge is a deeper understanding of this gospel. We must never remain at the same level of understanding of the gospel that we had when we were converted. Let's face it: most of us had min-imal knowledge of the gospel when we were saved. We were only ankle-deep, or at the most knee-deep, in the glorious truths of what the apostle Paul calls "the unsearchable riches of Christ" (Eph. 3:8). It is important that we keep growing in that knowledge.

We must also grow deeper in the knowledge of God Himself. The Bible is the self-revelation of God. In it we learn about the person and work of God. We need to grow in our appreciation of this book. There are many other religious books on the planet, so what makes the Bible unique? What is so special about it? You need to intelligently give a number of cogent arguments as to why this book is special, unique, and divine. Out of a prayerful reading and growing gratitude for this book should grow a deeper appreciation of God Himself.

We also need to have a deeper knowledge of the Christian life at a practical level. What does it mean to live a Christian life? How does one grow in his or her prayer life? How should a Christian live in the context of other believers in the church of Jesus Christ? What are the privileges and responsibilities of church membership? What does it mean to be a Christian husband or wife? How can I glorify God in my work? We need to continue growing in our understanding of all this.

We also need to have a growing understanding of the world in which we live. Remember, this is our Father's world. If you, as a believer, are to subdue the earth and have dominion over it (Gen. 1:28), you will need to grow in your knowledge of God's world.

No true spiritual growth takes place without engaging the mind. You must give yourself to the acquisition of knowledge. God's Word and His world are so vast that you can never arrive at the end of this knowledge. God Himself is an infinite being. As John Mason (c. 1646–1694) wrote in one of his hymns,

> How great a being, Lord, is thine,
> Which doth all beings keep!
> Thy knowledge is the only line
> To sound so vast a deep.
> Thou art a sea without a shore,
> A sun without a sphere;

Thy time is now and evermore,
Thy place is everywhere.[1]

We can study and study and study this great being and only scratch the surface. God's universe may not be infinite, but it is so vast that to us it appears infinite in terms of its width and depth. The more you study, the more you realize how little you know. But the only way you are going to grow is by a deliberate commitment to acquiring knowledge.

What Effect Does This Knowledge Have on Us?

When we grow in our spiritual knowledge, we find our assurance of salvation being strengthened. As the apostle Paul wrote to the Ephesians, "He Himself gave some to be apostles, some prophets, some evangelists, and some pastors and teachers, for the equipping of the saints for the work of ministry, for the edifying of the body of Christ, till we all come to the unity of the faith and of the knowledge of the Son of God, to a perfect man, to the measure of the stature of the fullness of Christ; that we should no longer be children, tossed to and fro and carried about with every wind of doctrine, by the trickery of men, in the cunning craftiness of deceitful plotting" (Eph. 4:11–14). He says that the reason Jesus gives teaching and preaching gifts to those in the leadership of the church is so they can build the church both quantitatively and qualitatively as they help believers attain a deeper knowledge of the Son of God. The phrase "the faith" in this text is not referring to the subjective element in us that enables us to apprehend or comprehend the things of God. Rather, it is referring to the truths that make up the Christian religion. For instance, the apostle Paul, referring to his early days as a preacher, said, "[The churches of Judea] were hearing only, 'He who formerly persecuted us now preaches the faith which he once tried to destroy.' And they glorified God in me" (Gal. 1:23–24). He was not preaching

---

1. John Mason, "How Shall I Sing That Majesty," Hymnary.org, accessed February 5, 2024, https://hymnary.org/text/how_shall_i_sing_that_majesty.

about the faculty in us that embraces spiritual truth. He was preaching the truth that makes up the Christian religion. Paul was saying that knowing this truth results in maturation "to the measure of the stature of the fullness of Christ." He says that one of the results of all this is that we may "no longer be children, tossed to and fro and carried about with every wind of doctrine, by the trickery of men, in the cunning craftiness of deceitful plotting." You become so grounded in Christian doctrine that as winds and waves of heresy are blowing and tossing in the real world—and they always will—you remain stable. Why? Because your anchor is deep, very deep, in the true knowledge of the ways of God and especially in the way of salvation.

This knowledge also enables us to have a balanced Christian life. Remember, we are talking about adding knowledge to virtue. It is possible for virtue to go off the rails and, in the process, make you a very unbalanced Christian. I think, for instance, of that person who wants to become a prayer warrior. Yet, because of unbalanced knowledge, such a person gives himself to prayer sessions at the expense of his family life. This can easily result in the breakdown of a marriage and family. Whereas the person is excellent in one area, they are a complete disaster in another. This can be prevented only when a person is growing in knowledge in all the areas of the Christian life. This results in a balanced believer.

Adding knowledge to virtue also prepares you to interpret trials and temptations in a godly way. Remember how Job understood the trial that befell him? With God's permission the Evil One literally destroyed everything that Job treasured, except his wife and his health. Job fell down on his knees and said, "Naked I came from my mother's womb, and naked shall I return there. The LORD gave, and the LORD has taken away; blessed be the name of the LORD" (Job 1:21). Here is my point: You do not acquire that knowledge the day the trial comes. You must know it before the trial, or you will go into a very serious depression and backslide. You must sink your anchor very deeply in the knowledge of God and His ways before Satan unleashes his arsenals on you. Only then will Satan fail to uproot you. Only then will you be able to speak as Job spoke.

Let us continue further in Job's account. In Satan's next attack, Job's health was taken away, to the extent that when his friends came to visit him, they could not speak for seven days as they saw the state in which they found him. Job was sitting in ashes and using broken pottery to scrape pus oozing out of the boils all over his body. This man who was once very rich and envied by his entire community was now in poverty and at the door of death. Job's wife became unhinged at that point. She said to him, "Do you still hold fast to your integrity? Curse God and die!" (Job 2:9). As far as she was concerned, it did not pay for Job to be faithful to such a God if He allowed all this to happen to him. Job answered her, "You speak as one of the foolish women speaks. Shall we indeed accept good from God, and shall we not accept adversity?" (2:10). In other words, should we serve God only when He is giving us what we want? Does He not have the right to do with our lives as He sees fit? That was not the kind of God Job's wife wanted, because she was deprived of the depth of knowledge that Job had of God's sovereignty.

There are many times when somebody claims to be a solid Christian until health problems begin. When he has gone to the hospital and has prayed but there is no improvement, you soon hear in our African context that the same person has gone to see a witch doctor and has sacrificed some chickens while standing half naked under the full moon in obedience to the instructions of the witch doctor to get healed. In the Western context and among the more educated ones in our African society, they disappear from church and show up at a faith healer's church, where they are told to sow a financial seed into the ministry in order to receive healing. How can true believers subject themselves to such charlatans? It is because they were not preparing for trials beforehand. Therefore, when trouble came, they were not ready for it. They were undone.

Joseph is yet another example. His brothers made him suffer. They wanted to kill him. They threw him in a well but finally decided to sell him as a slave. While he was serving as a slave in Egypt, the boss's wife falsely accused him of sexual molestation. As a result, he was thrown into prison. While in prison he helped a few people and asked them to remember him upon being released from prison. Well, they forgot about him. He must have been in prison for about ten years or so. Finally, one of them did remember Joseph, and he had him brought before Pharaoh. When Joseph interpreted Pharaoh's dream and found favor with him, he was released and was made the second most powerful man in the whole of Egypt. In God's providence, the very brothers who had wanted to kill him showed up looking for food from him. At that point most of us would have said, "I know that vengeance is the Lord's, but I think He may need a little help today." Not so with Joseph! He knew it was not really his brothers who had sent him to Egypt. It was God. Thus, after his father died, and his brothers concocted some story that Jacob had asked that Joseph should forgive his brothers, Joseph told them, "Do not be afraid, for am I in the place of God? But as for you, you meant evil against me; but God meant it for good, in order to bring it about as it is this day, to save many people alive" (Gen. 50:19–20). Joseph knew God. He knew that God governed history in His providence. He uses the worst situations to achieve a grand, positive, God-glorifying purpose in the end. Joseph was willing to leave everything in God's hands and worship Him. If we are to respond to trials the way Joseph did, without being bitter toward the individuals whom God uses to carry out His purposes, we must have a deeper knowledge of God.

When we grow in our spiritual knowledge, we also grow in our decision-making. We are better able to make right decisions for ourselves, our families, our work situations, and our church life. Life is made up of a lot of decisions. Like computer codes, these decisions take place in the background and produce answers that enable us to build our lives in one way or another. One of the reasons why our lives are chaotic is because we are not growing in our knowledge of God. We are unable to make decisions that are for the glory of God and the good of the people who depend on us.

Lastly, deeper knowledge gives you the ability to teach. Husbands should teach their wives (1 Cor. 14:35); parents should teach their children (Eph. 6:4); and, indeed, older believers should teach new believers (e.g., Titus 2:3). This is part of Christian discipleship. We are meant to pass on what we have learned to others (e.g., 2 Tim. 2:2). Many Christians back away from this responsibility due to their considerable lack of knowledge. If you are adding knowledge to virtue, it will keep you from being unfruitful. You will have something to teach others. The Christian faith is an intelligent faith. Give yourself intentionally to acquiring valuable knowledge and you will be able to teach others who need to grow in their knowledge of God and His ways.

A word of caution before we move on: Knowledge pursued for its own sake can have a negative effect by making us proud. The apostle Paul warned the Corinthians about this when he wrote, "Now concerning things offered to idols: We know that we all have knowledge. Knowledge puffs up, but love edifies. And if anyone thinks that he knows anything, he knows nothing yet as he ought to know. But if anyone loves God, this one is known by Him" (1 Cor. 8:1–3). If your pursuit of knowledge is going to benefit you spiritually, it must be motivated by love for God.

How Do We Add This Knowledge to Our Lives?

We acquire this knowledge, first of all, through our regular attendance at church meetings.

The gathered church is primarily meant to be an educational institution. The Lord Jesus Christ said, "Go therefore and make disciples of all the nations, baptizing them in the name of the Father and of the Son and of the Holy Spirit, teaching them to observe all things that I have commanded you; and lo, I am with you always, even to the end of the age" (Matt. 28:19–20). Notice how He says, "teaching them to observe all things that I have commanded you." We become familiar with truth by being committed to the regular meetings of the church. Set aside the Lord's Day for this purpose.

If your church has Bible study and two church services on this day, ensure that you are present for all of them. Take advantage of this opportunity. Distance or ill health or having very small children may forbid you from maximizing such an opportunity. That is understandable. Sadly, for too many believers, it is spiritual slothfulness that prevents them from making the most of what the Puritans used to call "the market day of the soul." People want to sleep in on the Lord's Day, and that cuts off the first meeting of the day. Then they want to watch sports on television in the evenings, and that cuts off the last meeting of the day. You cannot make spiritual progress like that. You must be intentional about maximizing attendance during teaching on the Lord's Day.

Unless you have a photographic memory, it is good to take notes while you are in service. Your notes do not need to be detailed, but they should at least provide you with some anchors to jog your memory. That way, when you have opportunity to review the day's teaching, you can do so from these notes. The lessons are meant to help you grow, but if you have already forgotten what you were taught, you will get very little profit from those lessons. Whatever method you use, make sure it helps you retain what is being taught.

When you go for Bible study, treat it like a study. Carry along a notebook and pen. Unless you are a genius, do not simply sit there and watch the lecturer or teacher as he or she teaches. You want to review the lessons and use the notes as if you were studying for your exams. Take notes that will be useful to you as you review afterward.

Apart from regular attendance at church meetings, you should also regularly read, deeply meditate on, and intelligently study the Scriptures on your own. Most of us are very busy. Life is hectic for all of us. But remember that you have a soul that needs daily manna from heaven. Do not depend on the manna you collect once a week. Gather it each day and feed your soul.

Finally, acquire and read Bible commentaries, Christian classics, biographies, historical books, and books on Christian living. You are treading where the saints have trod. For instance, if you are planning to get married or are already married, then read books on male-female relationships and how to sustain a godly marriage. Is your family growing? Well, collect books on how to raise godly children. Are you a church member? Get books about church life and read them so that you can be a responsible member of your congregation.

Do not be satisfied that you once acquired and read Christian books in your youth. Make this a lifelong habit. We all need to be stretched in our knowledge throughout our lives. On the eve of his execution, Paul wrote to Timothy, saying, "Bring the cloak that I left with Carpus at Troas when you come—and the books, especially the parchments" (2 Tim. 4:13). He recognized the importance of feeding the mind regularly. Take some of the money you normally spend on trivial things and use it on books instead. You can be sure you will be a better Christian because of this.

Develop the discipline of reading. Put aside time to read and guard it jealously. Line up some books you are interested in and discipline yourself to begin going through them in a year. You may not achieve your goal, but the discipline will help you to accomplish something. If you are married, talk with your spouse about what you are reading. Make it part of your fellowship in your marriage. Reading makes you an intelligent Christian. You are loving the Lord with your mind.

Let me end by saying again that the statement "Ignorance is the mother of devotion" does not apply to true Christianity. It is true of cults. A cult makes you a blind follower of the blind. It must not be so with you. If this generation is going to have spiritual giants who are going to impact the world, we will need intelligent and knowledgeable believers. You must aim to be one of them. May you long to know more about Jesus every day of your life, as we often sing in the hymn by Eliza Edmunds Hewitt (1851–1920):

> More about Jesus would I know,
> More of His grace to others show;
> More of His saving fullness see,
> More of His love who died for me.

More about Jesus let me learn,
More of His holy will discern;
Spirit of God, my teacher be,
Showing the things of Christ to me.

More about Jesus on His throne,
Riches in glory all His own;
More of His kingdom's sure increase;
More of His coming, Prince of peace.

More, more about Jesus,
More, more about Jesus;
More of His saving fullness see,
More of His love who died for me.[2]

---

2. Eliza Edmunds Hewitt, "More about Jesus," Hymnary.org, accessed February 5, 2024, https://hymnary.org/text/more_about_jesus_would_i_know_more_of.

CHAPTER 6

Master Your Desires

Giving all diligence, add…to knowledge self-control.
— 2 PETER 1:5, 6

Christianity is not simply a profession that you made at one point in your life. Christianity is life. It is new life, and consequently there ought to be growth. You ought to see over time that you are going from one degree of glory to another. The people around you should be able to testify to your spiritual progress as well.

This is the truth we are learning from 2 Peter 1. God has put several building blocks into the foundation of our lives as believers. Those realities are true about all of us who are God's children. He gave them to us from the point of our conversion. From there we grow in the spiritual realities Peter has been discussing. He emphasizes that we should have these in an ever-increasing measure because he knows that if we do, we are going to be fruitful and effective in our Christian lives.

The apostle Peter wants us to strain every muscle and sinew in our beings toward the goal of achieving greater levels of holiness. We have slowed down and are looking at each of these characteristics one by one. We have just looked at virtue and knowledge. In this chapter, we are moving on to self-control. Peter urges us to supplement our knowledge with self-control.

Self-control is applicable to the two areas we have covered so far: virtue and knowledge. Let us begin with the acquisition of knowledge. You must be very deliberate about several things if you are going to grow in knowledge. You will need self-discipline if, for instance, you are going to consistently gain knowledge through attending church services and Bible studies. You will also need to have mastery over yourself if you are seriously going to guard your time for reading Christian books.

Now let us see how self-control is related to virtue. Translating what you learn into virtue also demands self-control. In fact, this is where most people fail. They go to church and learn a lot about the Christian life. Yet they fail to apply what they learn to their lives. They are ever in a lax mode and so they never make progress. Where true spiritual knowledge has been properly acquired and applied, you can be sure that such a person also has the characteristic of self-control. This is what separates mature adults from children.

A Sinner's Lack of Self-Control

What does the term *self-control* mean? It refers to a person's mastery over his own appetites, especially his fallen and selfish desires. Such a person is able to say no to himself. Perhaps you've heard the story of a man who was in a supermarket doing some shopping. He was carrying a little boy with him. Those who were near kept hearing him say, "Charlie, no. No. Charlie, don't do it." Another shopper passed a comment, saying, "It sounds as if your little boy needs a tight rein on him." He responded, saying, "Actually, he is Tom. I'm Charlie." He was telling himself not to reach for the bottles of wine that were tempting to him. That might be a joke, but it makes the point. Self-control is saying no to yourself.

The King James Version uses the word *temperance* instead of *self-control* in our text. *Temperance* captures something of what is in the heart of the original Greek because it speaks about the ability to be balanced in all things. A self-controlled person is one who avoids reckless extremes. It suggests the ability to avoid excess.

The Bible teaches that the life of an unbeliever is characterized by a lack of self-control. We read, "Therefore gird up the loins of your mind, be sober, and rest your hope fully upon the grace that is to be brought to you at the revelation of Jesus Christ; as obedient children, not conforming yourselves to the former lusts, as in your ignorance" (1 Peter 1:13–14). Notice the language of self-control in verse 13: it speaks of preparing your mind for action and being sober-minded. You must not allow your mind to be swept away by your emotional state. In verse 14 Peter refers to the "former lusts." These are brutish emotions, corrupted desires that dictate fallen human life.

The apostle Peter wasn't alone in speaking about this. The apostle Paul, writing to the Galatians, says, "Now the works of the flesh are evident, which are: adultery, fornication, uncleanness, lewdness, idolatry, sorcery, hatred, contentions, jealousies, outbursts of wrath, selfish ambitions, dissensions, heresies, envy, murders, drunkenness, revelries, and the like; of which I tell you beforehand, just as I also told you in time past, that those who practice such things will not inherit the kingdom of God" (Gal. 5:19–21). Notice how so many of these works of the flesh are a result of recklessness. They result from a failure to control oneself. You lust after someone, and you start wanting to experience sexual pleasure with them. You are angry with someone, and you get into a fight. You attend a party, and you want to keep drinking alcohol until you are in a stupor. This is the non-Christian life. It is the work of the flesh.

Notice that half of the areas mentioned pertain to one's appetite for pleasure. It might be in terms of sex or food or strong drink. None of these are sinful in themselves. However, the failure to control their expression and indulgence is what often leads to sin. Idolatry may also be in terms of profit and wealth. The lack of self-control may exhibit itself in terms of the acquisition of cars and houses. You want more and more money to spend on yourself. This easily becomes a form of idolatry because money takes the place of God. As Jesus once said, "No one can serve two masters; for either he will hate the one and love the other, or else he will be loyal to the one and despise the other. You cannot serve God and mammon" (Matt. 6:24). Power and control, often at the expense of other people, are also listed among the works of the flesh. This is what often causes sorcery, enmity, strife, jealousy, fits of anger, rivalries, dissensions, divisions, and so on. It is the insatiable appetite to remain the winner in competition with other people in the church, in the community, and in the workplace. It may be due to a desire to make a name for oneself, which is driven by pride. That passion can be destructive to those who are blocking its way. This is a result of lack of self-control.

These are all characteristics of the non-Christian life. None of these things can ever bring you pardon from God or bring you into a true and loving relationship with Him. They can never finally bring you into heaven. The nonbeliever does not think beyond the grave. He says, "Let us eat and drink, for tomorrow we die!" (1 Cor. 15:32). It is total self-indulgence now and death tomorrow.

It is because of the absence of self-control that God, in His common grace, has provided institutions such as the state and family. They help to curb excesses through external restraints. With respect to sexual pleasure, for instance, the apostle Paul says that it is one of the reasons why God has given us the marriage relationship. He says, "To the unmarried and to the widows: It is good for them if they remain even as I am; but if they cannot exercise self-control, let them marry. For it is better to marry than to burn with passion" (1 Cor. 7:8–9). This counsel is for both believers and nonbelievers. Let us now turn to self-control among believers.

The Christian's Self-Control

We have already dealt with the relationship between virtue and knowledge in the previous chapter. Let us now look at the relationship between knowledge and self-control. As the Christian is studying what life really is and drinking in the reality of the God who governs the universe, he is better understanding who he is with respect to this world and with respect to this God. As he appreciates God's agenda across history and realizes that his business is to fit into this grand design, he begins to have a sense of purpose. It is this sense of purpose that the non-Christian does not have. This changes everything and it is what necessitates self-control in the believer.

The difference between a non-Christian and a Christian in this matter can be likened to two individuals who go to a party. One is an athlete who is preparing for a major tournament, and the other is his friend. As they approach the table laden with various well-prepared foods, the way each person thinks will be totally different. The athlete will be counting the calories and therefore skipping some of the most tempting dainties. He will be exercising a lot of self-control because he knows that he will have to do his best to burn off any extra calories that he consumes that night. It will mean a few more exercises over the next day or two. As for his friend, the main thought is that he must enjoy as much of this free food as he can. There are delicacies on those tables he has not tasted in a long time. Why should he miss the opportunity? You see, the athlete has knowledge and perspective that his friend does not have. Thus, they approach the table differently. It is the same between the Christian and the non-Christian. The Christian has the knowledge of God, which the non-Christian does not have. As a result, they approach life in different ways. The Christian exercises self-control because of that knowledge, while the non-Christian says, "Let us eat and drink, for tomorrow we die!"

The challenge is that when the Lord saves us, although our spirits undergo a rebirth, we still carry with us the fallen nature in the flesh. This is why the battle for self-control takes place. The apostle Paul speaks about this to the Galatians: "Walk in the Spirit, and you shall not fulfill the lust of the flesh. For the flesh lusts against the Spirit, and the Spirit against the flesh; and these are contrary to one another, so that you do not do the things that you wish" (Gal. 5:16–17). Each one of us possesses a fallen nature even after our conversion, which continues to point in the direction of selfishness, self-centeredness, and self-gratification. It is a daily battle for us to say no to the flesh and to win that fight.

The Lord Jesus Christ warned His followers to beware of a lack of self-control. He said to them, "But take heed to yourselves, lest your hearts be weighed down with carousing, drunkenness, and cares of this life, and that Day come on you unexpectedly" (Luke 21:34). Notice that He was saying this to His disciples. It is possible for believers to get so bogged down with the temporal things of this world. Jesus speaks about carousing, drunkenness, and the cares of this life. He warns against wild living. Such a life is never ready for death or for the second coming of Christ, which will come suddenly. It is possible to get carried away with things that have no eternal value while you have full health and then think about eternity only when it is too late. That is a result of lacking self-control.

The apostle Peter made a similar appeal in his first epistle. He wrote,

> Therefore, since Christ suffered for us in the flesh, arm your-selves also with the same mind, for he who has suffered in the flesh has ceased from sin, that he no longer should live the rest of his time in the flesh for the lusts of men, but for the will of God. For we have spent enough of our past lifetime in doing the will of the Gentiles—when we walked in lewdness, lusts, drunkenness, revelries, drinking parties, and abominable idol-atries. In regard to these, they think it strange that you do not run with them in the same flood of dissipation, speaking evil of you. They will give an account to Him who is ready to judge the living and the dead (1 Peter 4:1–5).

Christians should be differentiated from non-Christians due to this sense of temperance. Christians must have self-control and modera-tion in all things. Why? Peter says it is because Christ suffered in the flesh. Christians should arm themselves with the same way of think-ing, for whoever has suffered in the flesh has ceased from sin. Thus, Christians should live the remainder of their lives not for human passions but for the will of God.

This new life amazes unbelievers, who lack this knowledge. Peter says that they are surprised when you do not share in their debauchery, and as a result they malign you. The point is quite simple: One of the ways nonbelievers distinguish you from themselves is self-control. They notice that you do not allow your fallen passions to drive you. You think in terms of what God desires of you. That is what drives you.

We Achieve Self-Control by Putting on Christ

Self-control does not just happen. It is something you gain in an ever-increasing measure. We saw this in Galatians 5. It is a fruit of the Spirit. When you are converted to Christ, the Holy Spirit comes to take residence in you, and He enables you by His power to say no to all ungodliness and worldly passions. That is why you never pat yourself on the back when you notice spiritual progress in your life. You know that this progress is due to the presence and working of the Holy Spirit in you. He is the one who enables you to be who you are now.

What enables one believer to exhibit self-control in his life, while another believer, despite the Holy Spirit being in him, remains a victim of his own tumbling passions and emotions? It is what the apostle Paul calls "putting on Christ." The apostle Paul wrote, "Let us walk properly, as in the day, not in revelry and drunkenness, not in lewdness and lust, not in strife and envy. But put on the Lord Jesus Christ, and make no provision for the flesh, to fulfill its lusts" (Rom. 13:13–14). In other words, the more of Christ you have in your life, the less you feed your fallen nature or allow it to drive you.

To put on Christ involves recognizing the person and presence of God within you, and that happens only as you continue feasting on Him. You need to study Christ and His work. You need to enjoy the unsearchable riches of Jesus in your life. As you recognize that your only hope of forgiveness is in Him, it will drive you to go to Him again and again for pardon. As you acknowledge the reconciliation you now have with the living God because of Christ, you will treasure that fellowship. There is nothing in the whole universe like walking with God in this life. This fellowship has also given you brothers and sisters in Christ. We are one big happy family. Why? Because of Christ.

Add to all this the transformation that Jesus brings into your life as He makes you into a new creature who loves righteousness and hates sin. You love the worship of the living God and appreciate who this God is, and, consequently, you want to live for Him. Jesus continues to perform this work in you every day of your life. Add to all this the strength that He gives you in your moments of temptation, trials, and sorrow. Jesus is the all-sufficient one in the midst of all this. And that is not all. Jesus has also included you as a coworker with Him in the expansion of His kingdom. He has made you to participate in it according to the various gifts He has given you. That is glorious!

This brings us to the ultimate thought that brings us comfort as we face the last enemy—death. We can look forward to our rewards in glory, which can be ours only because of Christ. That causes light to shine on one's deathbed. You will say to whoever is crying for you on that day, "Don't cry for me, my friend. I'm heading home to my eternal reward. I have labored every day with this day in mind. I'm now going to meet my Savior and my God. He is the one I had fellowship with here by faith, as in a glass dimly. I'm now going to be with Him, to see Him face-to-face, and to enjoy His eternal presence. I am looking forward to hearing the words from His lips, saying, 'Well done, good and faithful servant.'"

The more you dwell on Christ, the more you put on Christ in your mind and heart. The more you do this, the more you enjoy these glorious truths of Christ, and the flesh is less able to find room to grow in your soul. You are full of Christ. The pleasures of this world grow strangely dim. They take a lesser place in your life. The moments of temptation will always be there, but they do not have the strong pull they once had on you, because you are full of God! That was how Joseph withstood Potiphar's wife when she was trying to tempt him to sleep with her. He was full of God. He said to her, "Look, my master does not know what is with me in the house, and he has committed all that he has to my hand. There is no one greater in this house than I, nor has he kept back anything from me but you, because you are his wife. How then can I do this great wickedness, and sin against God?" (Gen. 39:8–9). What can a moment of pleasure give compared to what would be lost in one's fellowship with God? Joseph was full of the joy of the Lord, which was his strength. That was what helped to keep him sane when he was so far away from kith and kin. Yes, he was a slave, but because God was with him, he was as good as a prince during all this. He could not bring himself to sin against God with all that knowledge treasured up in his soul.

Make every effort to add self-control to your knowledge. Remember that with spiritual growth there is no arriving at perfection on this side of eternity. To finally reach the stature of Christ is impossible. Our job is to continue seeking to be more like Him. We should pray to that end. As one hymn says,

> They are watching you
> Marking all you do,
> Hearing the things you say
> Let them see the Savior
> As He shines in you
> Let His power control you every day[1]

We should all be praying, "Let His power control me every day." The world has thrown God aside. Unbelievers are living in recklessness, and whatever their fallen nature tells them to do, they do. They are watching us and marking all we do. They are hearing the things we say. Let them see that we live under Jesus's sway, under His control. Let them see the Savior as He lives in us and as His power controls us every day. May we all exhibit that self-control to the praise and glory of His name. Amen!

---

1. "They Are Watching You," Lyrics Hymn, accessed February 5, 2024, https://lyricshymn.com/library/golden-bells/they-are-watching-you.

CHAPTER 7

Persevere to the End

Giving all diligence, add…to self-control perseverance.
—2 PETER 1:5, 6

At the time of writing this book, I have been a Christian for more than forty years. Looking back over those years reminds me of the importance of steadfastness. I recall in the early years of my walk with Christ that many of my peers were professing the Christian faith. It was like a revival! If the rate at which people were coming to Christ at that time had continued, we probably would have a different Zambia by now. The Christian churches certainly would be different. Many of those who sang God's praises with us are still alive, but their stories are very sad. Somewhere along the way, they stopped growing and went into decline. They stopped adding virtue to faith, knowledge to virtue, self-control to knowledge, and perseverance to self-control. They are now nothing more than cautionary examples to warn today's younger believers not to go in their direction.

Sadly, the same may be said today. Many individuals who are currently showing a lot of potential and promise in every area of the Christian faith will ultimately prove lacking in this one area—perseverance. Twenty to thirty years from now, their lives will exhibit the same decline. This is why it is so important to study this subject of perseverance. The apostle Peter says to add perseverance to self-control. Let us see what he has in mind as he exhorts believers to do just that.

What Perseverance Means

One way we can understand a word is simply by looking at its synonyms. *Perseverance* can be replaced with *steadfastness, endurance, patience,* and *constancy*. Conversely, we also appreciate a word by looking at its antonyms, its opposites. The opposite of *persevere* is captured by terms like *uncertain, shaky, wavering, unreliable,* and *faltering*. That helps you to imagine what Peter is saying here. He is telling believers that they should not be wavering and unreliable.

The Greek word used in the original text is *hupomeno*, which means "to remain under." In this case, it means to be constant under pressure. Those who frequent the gym to build their muscles know what this means. They lift weights and push themselves to continue their workout, even when their muscles are screaming for rest. Those who are weaker take breaks more frequently and finish their workout early. They fail to endure. Those who remain under the pressure for much longer become stronger because of their perseverance. This spiritual quality is a fruit of self-control and hence the connection that we have in this text. It means a firm commitment to endure over the long haul, despite pain and suffering.

Most of us can run. If we were being asked to run between one lamp post and the next, even an old man could do that. However, if we were being asked to run between two cities in a marathon, only a few would make it to the end. This is not about how fast you run but how far you run. That is what is being spoken about here in terms of continuing to grow in the Christian life until our race on earth is done. That is what perseverance is all about.

The Christian's Perseverance

How do we apply this to the Christian life? Let us begin with some bad news. Temptations and trials will never stop throughout your life here on earth. They will continue to beat against your soul until you die. This is where perseverance comes into the picture. In other areas of life, you can look forward to a clearly defined end point.

When you're in school, you anticipate your graduation day, when you can forever put aside all the pressure of exams and assignments. At some point in your career, you retire and can enjoy the benefits of your sweat for the rest of your life. No need to wake up early and feel the pressure of meeting deadlines. However, with respect to temptation and trials, this will never happen. That is truly bad news.

Imagine that you have been a Christian for five years and you are looking at people who have been believers for about three decades. It is very easy for you to look at the temptations and trials you are going through and imagine that perhaps upon getting beyond your tenth or twentieth year of walking with the Lord, those pressures will be over. You imagine that older Christians won the victory long ago and are now simply gliding toward heaven. Nothing could be further from the truth.

Perseverance means never giving up and giving in to Satan's temptations and to the world's trials. You must never finally yield. Rather, you must add perseverance to self-control. We all can exercise self-control for one day. Maybe even for one week or one month. Peter is saying we must go beyond that. We must persevere to the very end of our lives. Our spiritual growth should be a life-long pursuit.

Imagine a young Christian lady who is single. She gets a new job at a company and immediately catches the attention of a number of men in her new workplace. She makes it clear from the very first day that she is a Christian who loves the Lord. Despite that claim, one non-Christian man is determined to break through that barrier and date her. Initially, as soon as she notices his inordinate attention, she does not even want to entertain a conversation with him. But he does not give up. In due season, she begins to entertain his jokes and his compliments. As the year wears on, he starts to use charming words when addressing her and she simply giggles back. He offers her lifts to her home and often suggests that he comes up for a cup of tea. She finally agrees, and the rest is history. What has happened here? Her initial resistance and self-control eroded. A few months later, her church elder is listening to her saying that she wants to get married to this man whom she knows very well is not a Christian. She knows what the Bible says about the unequal yoke, but she still wants to go ahead and marry him. Perhaps by this time, she may even be pregnant from the same man. She failed to be steadfast in the midst of temptation. Initially, she was self-controlled, but that self-control failed to last.

The reason we yield to pressure is because we have been carrying a weight for such a long time, and our spiritual muscles finally give in. They have been screaming for rest from this temptation for some time, and Satan will not relent until disaster befalls you. You lower your moral standards—your spiritual virtues—in order to have some respite, but that is the beginning of the end. You begin to justify lowering the bar by referring to and comparing yourself with many Christians around you who live in compromise and sin. You also start accusing God of failing you. The young woman in our example might say, "If He really loved me, why did He not bring me a godly man? I have waited and prayed for such a long time, with no results from God. I sincerely wanted to have an excellent Christian marriage. God was not delivering on His promise. So, I have opted for something in between. A non-Christian man to marry me is better than continuing to be single for the rest of my life and experiencing pressure from all kinds of men. I am tired of waiting."

James addresses this very matter. He writes, "Therefore be patient, brethren, until the coming of the Lord. See how the farmer waits for the precious fruit of the earth, waiting patiently for it until it receives the early and latter rain. You also be patient. Establish your hearts, for the coming of the Lord is at hand…. Indeed we count them blessed who endure. You have heard of the perseverance of Job and seen the end intended by the Lord—that the Lord is very compassionate and merciful" (James 5:7–8, 11).

We also know the story of Job. He literally lost everything he had, even his children, but in the midst of his pain of loss, he said, "Naked I came from my mother's womb, and naked shall I return there. The LORD gave, and the LORD has taken away; blessed be the name of the LORD" (Job 1:21). Later, his friends came to comfort him but ended up being as useful as holes in a bucket. They only made his suffering worse by accusing him of wrongdoing. Yet, in the midst of his suffering, and some of the ill-advised statements that he made, we find some real gems of faith. Job was certainly steadfast. On one occasion, he cried, "For I know that my Redeemer lives, and He shall stand at last on the earth; and after my skin is destroyed, this I know, that in my flesh I shall see God, whom I shall see for myself, and my eyes shall behold, and not another. How my heart yearns within me!" (Job 19:25–27). He was determined to persevere to the very end as he fixed his heart and mind on the fact that his Redeemer lived and that because of that he would see God. The example of Job is a challenge to us today.

By persevering in his trial, Job actually grew spiritually. He grew in his knowledge and appreciation of who God was. When the period of Job's trial was coming to an end, God challenged him about the way he had begun to question divine wisdom. God said that Job was behaving as if he would have done a better job had he been the one governing the universe. God asked him where he was when creation was coming into existence. He also asked Job where he is each day when various creatures in God's world look for their provision. In the end, Job acknowledged that through this experience he now knew God better. Job said to God, "I know that You can do everything, and that no purpose of Yours can be withheld from You.... I had heard of You by the hearing of the ear, but now my eye sees You; therefore I abhor myself, and repent in dust and ashes" (Job 42:1–2, 5–6). That is how steadfastness not only enables us to be self-controlled over the long haul but also makes us better Christians.

We need to be consistently growing in our faith, excellence, knowledge, and self-control. The trajectory of our spiritual lives should be ever upward, despite a few bumps along the way. Anyone who is with you for a long time should be able to see that you are a consistently growing Christian.

We must be deliberate about this. That is why you should buy and read Christian books. That is why you should set aside time to read your Bible and pray daily. That is why you should schedule your time around fellowship with other believers. You know that you need that extra heat from other saints who are walking with God so you can be challenged to continue growing. You know that this demands time and effort, and you are willing to pay that price so you continue to grow. Sadly, this spiritual consistency is not common.

How to Add Perseverance to Self-Control

How does a Christian add steadfastness to his life? Godly perseverance grows out of faith, virtue, knowledge, and self-control. You cannot be steadfast, for instance, if you have not been practicing self-control. Anyone who has ever made real progress in physical exercise will tell you that when their muscles are screaming for rest, they will keep pushing themselves and pushing themselves until they've completed the workout they planned for that day. They have mastered their ability to say no to themselves until they've hit their goal. That is self-control, and perseverance grows out of the soil of that repeated discipline.

Another reality is that steadfastness grows out of knowledge. The apostle Paul wrote to the Romans, saying, "Not only that, but we also glory in tribulations, knowing that tribulation produces perseverance; and perseverance, character; and character, hope" (Rom. 5:3–4). The apostle makes the claim that Christians can rejoice in their suffering because they have a certain knowledge. What is that knowledge? It is grasping the fact that suffering produces endurance.

We also see the same point being made by James. He writes, "My brethren, count it all joy when you fall into various trials, knowing that the testing of your faith produces patience. But let patience have its perfect work, that you may be perfect and complete, lacking nothing" (James 1:2–4). That "knowing" that James talks about enables the Christian to count trials as a joy. He or she knows that the trial produces a better Christian. Without this knowledge, the Christian would despair.

Consider a woman whose husband is giving her trouble in the home. Where is this trouble coming from? Is it from the husband? Yes, it is. It is also from the devil. However, if she stops there, she will fail to persevere. She needs to go to a deeper level. She needs to have the knowledge that God has allowed this situation to happen for her own good. If she fails to see God's hand in her troubles, she will be bitter against her husband and end up sinning against him and against God.

Remember how Joseph was sold as a slave in Egypt. A time came when the tables were turned, and his brothers stood as beggars before him while he was the second most powerful man in Egypt. If he had been bitter because of what they had done to him, that would have been his opportunity to annihilate them. In fact, his brothers thought that he was simply waiting for his father to die before taking revenge, and so they cooked up a story that Jacob had left word that Joseph should pardon his brothers. How did Joseph respond to all this? He said, "Do not be afraid, for am I in the place of God? But as for you, you meant evil against me; but God meant it for good, in order to bring it about as it is this day, to save many people alive. Now therefore, do not be afraid; I will provide for you and your little ones" (Gen. 50:19–21). Joseph's steadfastness in being a benevolent person even to his brothers and their families was because of his knowledge of God's sovereignty and love. It must be the same with us. If we do not grow in our knowledge of the God of providence, we will fail to persevere in trials.

Jesus must be our model of excellence. The writer of the letter to the Hebrews refers to Jesus having a certain knowledge, which enabled Him to endure the cross valiantly. He says, "[We should be] looking unto Jesus, the author and finisher of our faith, who for the joy that was set before Him endured the cross, despising the shame, and has sat down at the right hand of the throne of God" (Heb. 12:2). The joy that was set before Jesus refers to His glorification and the final reward of His redemptive work. It was at the forefront of His mind as He went to Golgotha, and thus it fueled His determination to endure the cross. Even for us, the knowledge of the rewards awaiting us in glory should put grit into our being and enable us to persevere in trials. We also find the apostle Peter using this point as he urged suffering Christians in his own day: "For to this you were called, because Christ also suffered for us, leaving us an example, that you should follow His steps: 'Who committed no sin, nor was deceit found in His mouth'; who, when He was reviled, did not revile in return; when He suffered, He did not threaten, but committed Himself to Him who judges righteously" (1 Peter 2:21–23). Jesus concentrated on God as His final vindicator. This is what made Him victorious during His earthly trial on the eve of going to the cross. He must be our model. When we have this knowledge in us, it helps us to persevere in the midst of all our trials.

The lack of steadfastness that has characterized so many Christians must not be true of you. You must not end up a cautionary example that serves as a warning for the next generation of believers. Sadly, too many professing believers I started my Christian life with remind me of shattered ships that are now in the dockyard. They have not sunk to the depths of the sea, but neither are they carrying any goods across the oceans. They failed to persevere because of their lack of steadfast self-control when waves of temptations and trials continually pounded against them.

Tomorrow's church needs mature and godly leaders who have been tested and tried by temptations and have come out the other side with a stronger walk with God. Yes, tomorrow's church needs missionaries and pastors who will keep God's message before the world and embody it in their lives. That will not happen without the virtue of steadfastness. May today's believers rise to the challenge of being steadfast. If that happens, we will have a brighter tomorrow.

CHAPTER 8

The Source and Foundation of Godliness

Giving all diligence, add…to perseverance godliness.
— 2 PETER 1:5, 6

We now turn to the next imperative, adding godliness to our perseverance. Godliness is ultimately the summary of experiential Christianity. Everything that we need to realize this is provided for us by the power of God. This is what we learned from the apostle Peter in verse 3, where he wrote, "His divine power has given to us all things that pertain to life and godliness." No Christian should look at other believers who are exhibiting spiritual maturity and fruitfulness and say, "I admire the way those Christians live and serve the Lord. However, I was never meant to reach such levels of spiritual maturity. For me, it is enough to keep struggling with my darling sins." Such a view is unbiblical. God has provided every believer with what they need for spiritual maturity by His power.

There is nothing that captures the Christian life more than godliness. If there is one comment that those closest to you should make about you, it is that you are godly. If you are married, that is what your spouse should say about you, if you are truly mature in Christ. That is what Jesus Christ shed His blood and died for, to make you like Him. It was for that goal that He left the sacred throne in heaven to come and live in this gutter of sin. He wanted to bring you into this glorious state of godliness. Going to church is not an end in itself but rather a means of leading you into and keeping you in this state of godliness. Let us investigate this a little more.

Where Godliness Is in the Text

First, I want us to see where the word *godliness* is placed in Peter's list of spiritual qualities. If godliness is what I have said it is—the summary of the whole Christian life—then surely godliness must be at either the beginning or the end because the pursuit of it ought to motivate us in everything we do. It is the fountain from which our virtue, knowledge, self-control, and perseverance spring. Godliness should also be the final product in our lives once we have developed these qualities. So why does Peter throw it into the middle of this list?

Here is my suggested answer. This list of spiritual qualities is like climbing a mountain. Adding virtue, knowledge, self-control, and perseverance is making our way up to the mountaintop. Godliness is the top itself. The last two qualities in this list—brotherly kindness and love—are found as we descend the mountain. They are what should flow from a genuinely godly life. They speak about how a truly godly person relates to fellow believers and to the rest of the world. The relationship to both is one of love. So in reaching the spiritual quality of godliness, we have reached the mountaintop.

Who We Are and Who God Is

To understand godliness, we must begin with an understanding of who God is and who we are in relation to Him. Perhaps the best place to start is by looking at the first of the Ten Commandments. Exodus 20:1–3 says, "And God spoke all these words, saying: 'I am the LORD your God, who brought you out of the land of Egypt, out of the house of bondage. You shall have no other gods before Me.'" That is where godliness begins. It begins with God securing the unrivaled highest place in our lives. This is what He demanded from the Israelites, and it remains His chief demand on us today.

Godliness begins with the realization of who you truly are. First, you are a creature made by God and therefore are accountable to Him. You must live for God and not for yourself. This principle is true about everything in the world. There is nothing that is ever made by human beings, for instance, that is made for itself. Think about it. Nothing you have ever made—even if it was a toy car in your childhood—was ever made so that it could enjoy itself. It was always for your pleasure. When it began to fail to do its job, you were disgruntled with it and made plans to replace it with another one. It is the same between God and us. He created us for His own pleasure. We are accountable to Him.

Second, you are sinful. You were born a sinner and grew up in sin. Even after your conversion, you still struggle with sin. It is the one thing that causes you to shed bitter tears at the end of the day. You recognize that you are not where you want to be in the eyes of the One before whom you are accountable.

Finally, you are mortal. You will soon die. People will one day gather around a coffin, and you will be its occupant. Your life on earth will be over and you will go to meet Him to whom you must finally give an account of your life on earth.

If these three realities about you are clouded over by some worldly philosophy, you had better wake up before it is too late! You cannot be godly unless these three realities about you are the very atmosphere that you breathe daily: you are a creature made by God and are accountable to Him; you are a sinful, fallen creature; and you are a creature who must soon pass away.

But what about this God? Who is He? He is the exact opposite of the three realities we have considered about ourselves. It is because of this vast difference that He says, "You, My fallen creatures, My mortal creatures, shall have no other gods before Me. I must be the ultimate sovereign in your life." Who is God? He is the infinite one who can never be measured. He is the eternal one who has no beginning or end, who will never die. He is absolutely the independent one who does not need anything outside Himself for His own sustenance or fulfillment. He is the unchangeable one who never grows old or gets tired. He is the all-wise God who never makes a mistake. He is the all-knowing one and so has absolute knowledge concerning all things. He is all-powerful and can, at a snap of His fingers, disintegrate the whole universe into nothing. He is holiness itself, and thus holiness is to be measured by His standard. He is apart from the whole of His creation and indeed apart from all sin. He is just, and so He must punish sin. He is also good. Thus, He is a God of mercy, a God of love, and a God of grace.

This is the God who has made the universe—the God who owns it, preserves it, governs it. Not a single event in the whole of human history could ever happen without His permission. There is nothing that can happen in the kingdom of birds in the air or ants on the ground or fish in the sea without His bidding. This is the One who will come and judge the living and the dead. This is how God is described in the Bible.

Taking This God as Our God

Godliness is making this God your Lord and the chief object of your affections. It is living every day in light of this reality. Upon realizing that you are a sinful, mortal creature accountable to God, you cry out to Him that He might save you before you die. You are painfully conscious that if you continue living as you have been since birth, you will perish forever in the flames of hell. You seek God to save you from your sin. Thankfully, as we have already seen, this is a God who saves because He is good, merciful, loving, and gracious. He has given His very best, His only Son, who is infinitely more valuable than all the angels in heaven as a means of your salvation. He has nailed Him on a cruel cross to pay the price of your salvation. That is where godliness starts, at the foot of the cross. There is no godliness without salvation first. You can be religious and say your daily prayers, but until you have come to the foot of the cross as a hell-deserving sinner to plead with almighty God in the name of His Son to have unmerited mercy on you, you can never be godly.

Have you come to God in that way? Have you come to Him with the realization that if He does not save you, you are doomed? Have you seen something of God's glory, majesty, and holiness and thus cried out like Isaiah the prophet, "Woe is me, for I am undone! Because I am a man of unclean lips, and I dwell in the midst of a people of unclean lips; for my eyes have seen the King, the LORD of hosts" (Isa. 6:5)? For you to embrace true godliness, you must let go of your own self-righteousness and pray to God, saying in the words of Augustus Toplady,

> Nothing in my hand I bring,
> Simply to the cross I cling;
> Naked, come to thee for dress;
> Helpless, look to thee for grace;
> Foul, I to the fountain fly,
> Wash me, Savior, or I die.[1]

You never become a true Christian until you reach such levels of self-emptiness and until you refuse to be comforted unless God Himself comforts you. When He does so, the joy and peace that fill your heart are amazing. There is nothing like that in the world. To know that God has pardoned you of all your transgressions is a slice of heaven on earth. You experience a peace that surpasses all understanding and that enables you to sing, "It is well with my soul." You experience the joy that made Christian in *The Pilgrim's Progress* jump into the air with three leaps when the burden he had been carrying in the City of Destruction finally fell off his shoulders and rolled into the open grave at the foot of the cross.

It is this joyful and peaceful atmosphere in the soul that enables a truly godly person to yield to God's revealed will. This person will want to do anything the Bible says he should do. When you see individuals who claim to be Christians but who want to summon God to a negotiating table before they will yield to His demands, there is

---

1. Augustus Toplady, "Rock of Ages," Hymnary.org, accessed February 6, 2024, https://hymnary.org/text/rock_of_ages_cleft_for_me_let_me_hide.

something seriously amiss there. A sinner who knows he deserves to perish forever but has received God's mercy will want to surrender unreservedly to Him. Rather, he will say, "Whatever the Bible says, it is supreme over my life." He will not do so to attract the world's praise. Rather, it is because he has entered a relationship with the living God and wants to live for Him. This is the root of godliness.

This reality also makes such individuals gladly yield to God's providential administration in their lives. Sinners become frustrated when God takes away something that they cherish or refuses to give them something they desperately want. They feel as if they deserve something from God. They basically say to Him, "If You will not give this to me, I am going to another god to get it." A truly godly soul does not say that. Instead, he says to God, "You are my highest good. Take away my spouse, my children, my property, my health, or even take me to an early grave if You please. What I want above all things is for Your will to be done in my life if it draws me closer to You, my highest good." It was this godliness that enabled Horatio Spafford to write the hymn "When Peace like a River." He had lost his business as a lawyer, then his children in a ship accident. In reflecting on this, he wrote,

> When peace like a river attendeth my way,
> When sorrows like sea billows roll;
> Whatever my lot, thou hast taught me to say,
> "It is well, it is well with my soul."

> Though Satan should buffet, though trials should come,
> Let this blest assurance control:
> That Christ has regarded my helpless estate,
> And has shed his own blood for my soul.[2]

That is godliness. This happens only when God is made your highest good. That is what God meant when He commanded the children of Israel, "You shall have no other gods before Me" (Ex. 20:3). If they ensured He had an unrivaled place in their lives, even

---

2. Horatio Spafford, "When Peace like a River," Hymnary.org, accessed February 6, 2024, https://hymnary.org/text/when_peace_like_a_river_attendeth_my_way.

trials in the wilderness and in the promised land would not take them away from Him. It is the same with us today. Once we take this God to be our God, we will yield to His commands and to His providence. We will also live every moment of our lives wanting only one thing—that God might be glorified. Thus, godliness produces a passion for the honor of God. That is what motivates us to worship God at church, at home on our own, and with our loved ones in family worship. We are motivated to read our Bibles because we want to know God and how we can honor Him better.

The Outworking of This

How does godliness work itself out in our daily lives? We have seen that it commences when you cry out to God for salvation and experience the joy of having your sins forgiven. From there you yield your life to God's commands and His providential administration of affairs related to you. Your one desire in all this is that God might be glorified in everything you think, say, and do. You become an instinctive worshiper seven days a week. This is especially the case when you gather among the children of God on the one day He has set for His worship. You guard the Lord's Day because you want to worship Him.

As you gaze at the indescribable beauty of God's attributes as they shine through the Scriptures, you see in Him a beauty that shines brighter than the sun—a beauty of such magnificence that it makes the beauty of flowers and of birds look utterly colorless. Yes, the beauty of the whole of creation is only a pale reflection of the One who created it. As one chorus says,

> Turn your eyes upon Jesus,
> Look full in His wonderful face,
> And the things of earth will grow strangely dim,
> In the light of His glory and grace.[3]

---

3. Hele Howarth Lemmel, "Turn Your Eyes upon Jesus," Hymnary.org, accessed February 6, 2024, https://hymnary.org/text/o_soul_are_you_weary_and_troubled.

As you look at all that beauty in the Scriptures, you want more fellowship with Jesus and want to be like Him. You want to be conformed to that image you are beholding with your spiritual eyes. As the apostle Paul wrote from prison to the church in Philippi, "That I may know Him and the power of His resurrection, and the fellowship of His sufferings, being conformed to His death" (Phil. 3:10). During all the trials and temptations brought to you by circumstances and by the malice of enemies, your chief desire is to become like the Lord Jesus Christ even as you experience fellowship with Him. You want to love Him who is infinitely lovable. Indeed, He loves you eternally and sacrificially. You want to reflect that love by loving Him back. He deserves your utmost love, trust, and obedience. That is what a godly soul desires. It is simply the fulfillment of the greatest command of all. The Bible says,

> Then one of the scribes came, and having heard them reasoning together, perceiving that He had answered them well, asked Him, "Which is the first commandment of all?"
>
> Jesus answered him, "The first of all the commandments is: 'Hear, O Israel, the LORD our God, the LORD is one. And you shall love the LORD your God with all your heart, with all your soul, with all your mind, and with all your strength.' This is the first commandment. And the second, like it, is this: 'You shall love your neighbor as yourself.' There is no other commandment greater than these." (Mark 12:28–31)

You can never in this life fully "love the LORD your God with all your heart, with all your soul, with all your mind, and with all your strength." You never get there, but true godliness remains in pursuit of that goal throughout this life. Anybody who is close enough to you cannot miss that this is your agenda in life—to love and serve this God to the very end. You long to hear the words, "Well done, good and faithful servant.... Enter into the joy of your lord" (Matt. 25:23). That is what true godliness is. It is the life God wants you to have.

CHAPTER 9

The Supreme Fruit
of Godliness

Giving all diligence, add…to perseverance godliness.
—2 PETER 1:5, 6

Many years ago, I worked in the Zambian copper mines. On one occasion, we had to build a crusher at the lowest level of the mine to crush the ore that was assigned for production. A lot of painstaking effort was put into getting the foundation of the crusher ready. Once it was tested and found to be able to withstand the pressure of the crusher that was to be erected on it, we all had an evening of celebrations. As important as that was, the next task was assembling the gigantic crusher underground. We watched with amazement as huge pieces of steel were taken underground, all the way to the lowest level of the mine. Engineers worked around the clock to put this together. Finally, the day came when it was put to the test and the first few pieces of broken-down ore were conveyed to the smelter on the surface.

The relationship between what I covered about godliness in the last chapter and what I am covering in this chapter can be likened to the foundation and the gigantic crusher that I have described. In the last chapter I discussed the source and foundation of godliness. It is a product of regeneration. We get to know who we are, who God is, and how we can be reconciled to Him. In this chapter, we are going to see the fruit of this crusher. What is it that arrives at the smelter and convinces us that there is a real crusher working underground?

With respect to godliness, we want to see what it looks like in the Christian life. How do believers grow in godliness, and what does the apostle Peter mean when he says, "Giving all diligence, add…to perseverance godliness"? I touched on this very briefly in the previous chapter, but now I want to open this up in more detail. I would like us to appreciate the effect of godliness in our lives and see what we should be and do so that our friends, spouses, and neighbors can see change in us and say, "That person is truly godly."

Supreme Love for God

The most obvious sign of true godliness is that your heart has a supreme love for God. We saw this in the previous chapter when Jesus spoke about the greatest of all commandments. Quoting from the Old Testament, He said, "You shall love the LORD your God with all your heart, with all your soul, with all your mind, and with all your strength" (Mark 12:30). The reason you will have this supreme love for God is because you have come to appreciate who you are relative to who He is. You are nothing but dust. Yet this glorious God who could have destroyed you because of your sin instead gave His own Son for you. Consequently, you are so full of gratitude for the God who has loved you this way. Those who are genuinely godly are in love with the living God. For them, salvation is not just a hellfire insurance policy. They truly love the Lord, and when they think of heaven they think in terms of going to be with the One whom they love.

Supreme Fear for God

Those who are truly godly do not just love God; they also fear Him. He is on His exalted throne in heaven, and we are down here on earth. When we realize that, we are filled with a wholesome fear. We realize that this is the God of judgment and wrath. He is holy and therefore must punish sinners. He knows all the details of our lives. He knows the words we speak in private and the thoughts we entertain in our minds. That alone makes us realize that we must be holy inside and out. The wise man in Ecclesiastes says,

> Walk prudently when you go to the house of God; and draw near to hear rather than to give the sacrifice of fools, for they do not know that they do evil.
>
>> Do not be rash with your mouth,
>> And let not your heart utter anything hastily before God.
>> For God is in heaven, and you on earth;
>> Therefore let your words be few....
>
>> When you make a vow to God, do not delay to pay it;
>> for He has no pleasure in fools....
>
> Do not let your mouth cause your flesh to sin, nor say before the messenger of God that it was an error. Why should God be angry at your excuse and destroy the work of your hands? For in the multitude of dreams and many words there is also vanity. But fear God. (Eccl. 5:1–2, 4, 6–7)

Truly godly people will not be hypocrites. What they fear most is not public opinion of themselves. These individuals do not conduct themselves well because they are near their parents, or because they have seen policemen, or because they have auditors visiting them shortly, or because elders are looking over their shoulders. Rather, they know there is an eye that sees everything they do. It is the eye of God. They fear Him with a wholesome fear. This is what makes them truly wise. The Bible tells us in Proverbs 9:10, "The fear of the LORD is the beginning of wisdom."

Supreme Trust in God

When you are godly, your heart has a supreme trust in God. Let me prove this. This world is unpredictable. Today you might have people smiling at you, but the next day the same people may want to destroy you. One moment you are well and the next moment you are unwell. A godly person is one who trusts that the God he has come to know is the God who is in control of everything in this universe. There is not a single hair that falls to the ground without Him permitting it. He is the all-powerful and all-knowing God. He is the faithful God with whom we are in a covenant. He will ensure that we arrive safely in heaven. Therefore, we can trust Him, whatever comes our way. Even when human beings who are more powerful than us rise against us, He will be our defender. Psalm 18:1–3 reads (starting with the prologue),

> To the Chief Musician. A Psalm of David the servant of the LORD, who spoke to the LORD the words of this song on the day that the LORD delivered him from the hand of all his enemies and from the hand of Saul. And he said:
>
> I will love You, O LORD, my strength. The LORD is my rock and my fortress and my deliverer; My God, my strength, in whom I will trust; my shield and the horn of my salvation, my stronghold. I will call upon the LORD, who is worthy to be praised; so shall I be saved from my enemies.

This godly man trusted the Lord, even though Saul, the most powerful man in the land, was after him. He cried to the Lord and the Lord rescued him.

Do you have this kind of trust? Peter is telling you to add godliness to your perseverance. One of the attributes of this godliness is trusting God in every circumstance of life. Psalm 27:1–3 says, "The LORD is my light and my salvation; whom shall I fear? The LORD is the strength of my life; of whom shall I be afraid? When the wicked came against me to eat up my flesh, my enemies and foes, they stumbled and fell. Though an army may encamp against me, my heart shall not fear; though war may rise against me, in this I will be confident." Too many professing Christians are filled with complaints instead of trust in the Lord. Trust includes fully and peacefully submitting to God's providences. You will have disappointments, illnesses, robberies, accidents, and so on. In all this, you will be able to say as Job did, "Naked I came from my mother's womb, and naked shall I return there. The LORD gave, and the LORD has taken away; blessed be the name of the LORD" (Job 1:21). God is still in control of all the details of your life.

That is godliness! You do not press the panic button when all hell breaks loose on your soul. You instead say that in the Lord's own time He will make all things beautiful. He is sovereign over all of life and knows what is happening to you. You trust God supremely.

Supreme Obedience to God

Godliness is an unflinching loyalty to God and His laws, commandments, and ordinances. As a result, you give obedience to Him in all areas of your life. This is the highest evidence of godliness. This was Jesus's aim in giving the Great Commission: "Go therefore and make disciples of all the nations, baptizing them in the name of the Father and of the Son and of the Holy Spirit, teaching them to observe all things that I have commanded you; and lo, I am with you always, even to the end of the age" (Matt. 28:19–20). The apostle Paul called this "obedience to the faith" (Rom. 1:5; 16:26), which the apostles were seeking to bring about through the preaching of the gospel.

False conversions fail to produce true godliness and therefore fail to produce lasting obedience. When temptations and trials come, such individuals go from obedience to disobedience. This was what Jesus had in mind when He taught the parable of the sower. He said, "But he who received the seed on stony places, this is he who hears the word and immediately receives it with joy; yet he has no root in himself, but endures only for a while. For when tribulation or persecution arises because of the word, immediately he stumbles. Now he who received seed among the thorns is he who hears the word, and the cares of this world and the deceitfulness of riches choke the word, and he becomes unfruitful" (Matt. 13:20–22).

An example of a dogged obedience that was willing to suffer or even die rather than be disobedient is seen in the apostles Peter and John when they said to the Jewish leaders, "Whether it is right in the sight of God to listen to you more than to God, you judge. For we cannot but speak the things which we have seen and heard" (Acts 4:19–20). Only true godliness in the soul, produced by the Word of God and the Spirit of God, can generate such a supreme obedience.

Supreme Worship of God

When you are godly, you want to give God your highest worship. Godliness begins with the realization that we are mortal and sinful creatures. Then our eyes of faith see something of the glory of God. That contrast makes us mesmerized worshipers of the living God. In the book of Revelation, John has a preview of what is done in heaven. He sees angelic beings speaking to God, saying, "You are worthy, O Lord, to receive glory and honor and power; for You created all things, and by Your will they exist and were created" (Rev. 4:11). That vision leaves him in a state of worship on the island of Patmos. We may not have been blessed with such a vision. Yet all we need to do to be carried into a state of worship is look at God's creation on earth. We do not even have to look at the planets, solar system, and galaxies. We simply have to look at how we have been kept alive for so many years. God has kept our hearts beating and has sustained the entire systems of life within us. That alone should make us true worshipers of God.

Where godliness is missing, men and women fail to worship Him. They would rather be at home watching sports than be with fellow believers worshiping God on the Lord's Day. Psalm 122:1 says, "I was glad when they said to me, 'Let us go into the house of the LORD.'" A godly soul longs to meet and worship with the people of God.

Supreme Hunger for God

A godly soul has a supreme hunger for God. I am often shocked when I hear a believer speak of being bored and lonely. As a believer, the one being you should want to be with is the Lord Himself. You should long for Him and want time alone so that you might spend it with the Lover of your soul, the altogether lovely One, your supreme joy. The psalmist testifies, "Whom have I in heaven but You? And there is none upon earth that I desire besides You" (Ps. 73:25). A godly person is someone who has found his or her supreme joy in knowing the Lord. Your primary reason for going to the house of God is to have fellowship with Him among His people. It is what you prize the most—this fellowship between your soul and God. It is what makes you run away from and hate sin. You fear that it will affect the fellowship you treasure with God. You know that sin grieves His Spirit. You desire to know God, to be conformed to His image. You want to be holy because He says, "Be holy, for I am holy" (1 Peter 1:16). When you become more and more like God, fellowship with Him is sweeter, and you want to be like Him in every way. You want to seek hard after God.

In Psalm 63:1–7, the psalmist says,

> O God, You are my God;
> Early will I seek You;
> My soul thirsts for You;
> My flesh longs for You
> In a dry and thirsty land
> Where there is no water.
> So I have looked for You in the sanctuary,
> To see Your power and Your glory.
>
> Because Your lovingkindness is better than life,
> My lips shall praise You.
> Thus I will bless You while I live;
> I will lift up my hands in Your name.
> My soul shall be satisfied as with marrow and fatness,
> And my mouth shall praise You with joyful lips.
>
> When I remember You on my bed,
> I meditate on You in the night watches.
> Because You have been my help,
> Therefore in the shadow of Your wings I will rejoice.

This is the longing of the soul of the godly man. The apostle Paul utters similar words in Philippians 3:10: "That I may know Him and the power of His resurrection, and the fellowship of His sufferings, being conformed to His death." These are not the words of a young convert. This is the apostle Paul, who has planted many churches and written many letters to edify the church. He speaks here about longing to know God and the power of His resurrection. That is godliness.

Godliness causes you to have a spiritual attitude toward the Bible. When you open it, you not only want lessons for life and living but also want the God whom you love to speak to you. You want Him to reveal Himself to you and meet with you in the pages of Scripture. You are hungering and thirsting for Him. Similarly, when you pick up a Christian book, it is because you want to think hard and stretch your mind more and more on the greatest subject in the universe—God Himself! This is what a real hunger after God looks like.

Lastly, part of this hunger for God is a desire to finally behold Him in eternity, when faith becomes sight and you hear Him say the words, "Well done!" You have read those words in Scripture, but you long to hear them in eternity from the One who has loved you with an everlasting love. You want to meet Him and be with Him forever.

This is Christianity. The apostle Peter wants you to let this quality of godliness grow and blossom until you arrive in glory. This is why the Lord saved you. It is not just to give you a ticket to heaven that you can keep in your pocket while passing through the mud and sewer of this world. Rather, it is for you to experience something of this reality of being like God. It is for you to be in this extraordinary relationship with Him. It is this reality that attracts the attention of the world to real Christianity. They see through everything else as hypocrisy and pretense because they can do it too. But this godliness is the only thing that they cannot reproduce through the arm of flesh. Only God can produce this.

In this chapter, I have sought to describe what is evident in a person who is godly. You see a supreme love for, fear of, trust in, obedience to, worship of, and hunger for God. When you are with a person who exudes these qualities, you walk away saying, "That person is godly." This is becoming so rare in our world today. So many are missing out on the life of God in the soul of man. They are missing out on true Christianity and on that which Jesus Christ shed His blood for them to experience here on earth and even more gloriously in heaven. The result is that they do not attract people to Christ. Their coworkers, children, and spouses admire very little about their lives. There is very little in them that pulls others heavenward. May it not be true of us. May our lives demonstrate the supreme fruit of godliness in an ever-growing way.

CHAPTER 10

Attaining Godliness

Giving all diligence, add…to perseverance godliness.
— 2 PETER 1:5, 6

After reading the last two chapters, you should be asking yourself, In a world that is so full of sin, how do I attain godliness? How can I become different from the rest of the world around me? As godliness was being described, it must have been plain to see that it does not grow on natural soil. It must be something that God alone produces in you. So how do you attain this? How do you become a spiritual giant in a world that cares nothing about spirituality? It is through the power of the grace of God and through the eye of faith. Let us examine each of these two.

By the Power of God

Godliness is a fruit of God's grace and power in our lives. We already noticed this from 2 Peter 1:3: "His divine power has given to us all things that pertain to life and godliness."

How has God's power given us what we need to be godly? It is by His grace. This is what the apostle Paul says in Titus 2:11–12: "For the grace of God that brings salvation has appeared to all men, teaching us that, denying ungodliness and worldly lusts, we should live soberly, righteously, and godly in the present age." Earlier in Titus 2, the apostle Paul had been instructing Titus to insist that God's people should be different from the people of the world, that they should live lives characterized by true godliness. In Titus 2:1 we read, "But as for you, speak the things which are proper for sound doctrine." He was not telling Titus to teach sound doctrine (he had already done that in chapter 1) but to teach what is in line with—what accords with—sound doctrine. Titus was to teach the kind of life that measures up to and is in line with the doctrine he was already teaching.

What does that life look like? This is what he spells out in verses 2–10. For instance, he wrote, "Older men be sober, reverent, temperate, sound in faith, in love, in patience" (v. 2). What about the women? "Older women likewise, that they be reverent in behavior, not slanderers, not given to much wine, teachers of good things— that they admonish the young women to love their husbands, to love their children, to be discreet, chaste, homemakers, good, obedient to their own husbands" (vv. 3–5). He also discusses younger men and bondservants (vv. 6–10). Titus himself was to be a good role model of all this in the way he carried out his teaching ministry.

In case some people thought that such a life was not possible for them, the apostle Paul argued that the grace of God was capable of producing such a life in "all men" (v. 11). There was no exception— whether young or old, male or female, slave or free. A moral power enabled them to renounce ungodliness and, in its place, empowered them to live godly lives. That was what Paul was instructing in Titus 2:11–15. Titus was to insist on believers being godly despite their ungodly environment.

We often limit God's grace to the realm of forgiveness. It is true that this is one of the most important manifestations of His grace. Through Christ He has given us the exact opposite of what we deserve. We deserved condemnation, but instead He has given us a free pardon. We deserved to die and go to hell, but instead He gave us His own Son to die in our place. This truth never grows stale in the soul of a believer. It always warms our hearts and inspires us to worship the God of grace. However, the grace of God is also an empowering energy that enables us to live a life which would have been impossible for us to live.

One example of this is the way in which Paul referred to the grace of God in his life in 1 Corinthians 15:8–10. Speaking about the resurrected Christ, he wrote, "Then last of all He was seen by me also, as by one born out of due time. For I am the least of the apostles, who am not worthy to be called an apostle, because I persecuted the church of God. But by the grace of God I am what I am, and His grace toward me was not in vain; but I labored more abundantly than they all, yet not I, but the grace of God which was with me." No one can doubt that Paul labored more than the other apostles. Half of the New Testament came from his pen! He probably planted more churches than the other apostles. Yet he realized and acknowledged that this extraordinary energy came from God.

Another example of this is found in 2 Corinthians 12, where the apostle Paul was pleading with God to take away the "thorn" in his flesh, whatever it was (v. 7). He said that he pleaded with the Lord three times until Jesus responded and said, "My grace is sufficient for you, for My strength is made perfect in weakness." Paul concluded, "Therefore most gladly I will rather boast in my infirmities, that the power of Christ may rest upon me" (v. 9). The context makes it plain that the issue here was not about pardon from sin but power to overcome weakness. The words *grace* and *power* are used interchangeably. God's grace enabled the apostle Paul to live victoriously despite the thorn in his flesh.

It is the same with us. At the point of our conversion, the grace of God is not just an external favor being given to us by way of forgiveness. It is also an internal energy from God that enables us to live to His glory. Paul tells Titus that this spiritual energy is given to everyone who is saved. It enables us to say no to worldliness and empowers us to live a life that is otherwise impossible. Those who are genuinely saved can live this kind of life as they wait "for the blessed hope and glorious appearing of our great God and Savior Jesus Christ, who gave Himself for us, that He might redeem us from every lawless deed and purify for Himself His own special people, zealous for good works" (Titus 2:13–14).

This is where we must start as we consider how to attain godliness. It is a product of the power of God in the human soul. If you have no real thirst for godliness, if your inner life cannot be differentiated from the unbelieving people around you, and if this energy toward moral transformation does not pulsate within you, then we should not expect you to seek further spirituality. In fact, I daresay you have never truly experienced God's salvation.

You may want to say you are converted. In the end, only God knows the heart. But the proof of the pudding is in the eating. When you are out there on your own amid an ungodly world that is pulling you downward, what is happening in your soul? Are you becoming like them or is there an internal energy that pulls you in a different direction? Does this result in you pushing away all the rubble that is thrown onto you, revealing a life that is completely different from the life of the world? Sadly, church leaders can be in such a hurry to see their church grow that as long as someone has said the sinner's prayer, they want them to quickly join church membership. These shallow "converts" are the ones who will hear Jesus say in the end, "I never knew you; depart from Me, you who practice lawlessness!" (Matt. 7:23). If Jesus has saved you from sin, it will show. Christianity is not a mere philosophy. It transforms a person's life from the inside out. Jesus fills them with His Spirit, who empowers them toward moral purity and thus enables them to live a life that is different from the world—a life of godliness, a God-centered life.

If your life does not exude this energy for godliness, the least you can do for yourself is to go back to the place where you thought you came to Christ in salvation and do some serious introspection. Could you have missed something? Go back to the foot of the cross and plead with the Lord Jesus Christ that He may truly save you if He has not done so already. Pray that His salvation in you may so shine that people around you will see its brilliance. Once they ask why you are so different, you too can say with the apostle Paul, "It is not me; it is the grace of God within me."

Grows Out of Faith

Having observed that godliness grows by the power of God through His grace, we will now move on to yet another source of this growth. It is the faith that God gives us at the point of our conversion. Godliness can flourish only in a soul that by faith is ever conscious of the reality of God. If we go back to 2 Peter 1, we see it is not only divine power that produces godliness but also the foundation of faith. In verse 1 of this chapter, the apostle Peter writes, "Simon Peter, a bondservant and apostle of Jesus Christ, to those who have obtained like precious faith with us by the righteousness of our God and Savior Jesus Christ." When we examined this verse closely in chapter 1, I mentioned that when the Bible is referring to doctrine, it uses the definite article before the word *faith*. When the definite article is missing, it refers to the subjective element in us that embraces the doctrine. It refers to actual faith. That is what Peter is referring to in this text. He is saying that the same faith that was planted in him is the faith that has been planted in every believer. All of us have the same foundation for our lives, and it is that same foundation on which we now begin to build.

Later, in verse 5, Peter says, "For this very reason, giving all diligence, add to your faith virtue." This faith has been there ever since you first became a Christian. God gave it to you. Now you are supposed to add to that faith all these other qualities of the Christian life—virtue, knowledge, self-control, perseverance, and godliness. This faith is the foundation on which godliness ultimately grows.

Faith is the ever-present consciousness of the reality of God. Hebrews 11:23–26 says of Moses, "By faith Moses, when he was born, was hidden three months by his parents, because they saw he was a beautiful child; and they were not afraid of the king's command. By faith Moses, when he became of age, refused to be called the son of Pharaoh's daughter, choosing rather to suffer affliction with the people of God than to enjoy the passing pleasures of sin, esteeming the reproach of Christ greater riches than the treasures in Egypt; for he looked to the reward." Moses was so privileged in Egypt and could have chosen to enjoy the world. Growing up in Pharaoh's palace, he had the best the world had to offer. Yet Moses had a certain reality or consciousness that was a fruit of faith. Because of that consciousness, he was willing to give up the palace and all its privileges and to suffer the consequences of that decision. His spiritual eyes saw Christ, and he knew that the reproach of Christ was better than the glittering gold of the palace. Verse 27 says, "By faith he forsook Egypt, not fearing the wrath of the king; for he endured as seeing Him who is invisible."

Later, there was an extraordinary experience that caused his faith to grow even more. While out in the desert, after he had run away from Pharaoh for dear life's sake, he saw a bush that was burning but not consumed. As he drew near, he heard the voice of God saying, "Come now, therefore, and I will send you to Pharaoh that you may bring My people, the children of Israel, out of Egypt" (Ex. 3:10). There is no doubt that this extraordinary experience went a long way toward making Moses into the man of God that he became. We may not have such out-of-this-world encounters, but as we experience God more and more in ordinary yet providential ways, it augments our faith and results in greater godliness.

Another experience Moses had in his walk with God was when he became totally demoralized by the stubbornness of the people of Israel while in the desert after God rescued them from Egypt. They were at Mount Sinai, and the people, together with Moses's brother, Aaron, succumbed to idolatry. Moses was on the verge of giving up. He pleaded with God, saying, "Please, show me Your glory" (Ex. 33:18). The Lord obliged and said, "I will make all My goodness pass before you, and I will proclaim the name of the LORD before you. I will be gracious to whom I will be gracious, and I will have compassion on whom I will have compassion" (v. 19). Although God did not allow Moses to see Himself directly, He caused His glory to pass by him. That experience with God enabled Moses to go the extra mile.

As unique as this experience was to Moses, we can nonetheless say that often our walk with God involves personal experiences that build our faith unto godliness. The reality of God is refreshed in our souls, and we are renewed in our resolve to live for Him. This is what makes a Christian stand out in a world of need and ungodliness. Perhaps in the home where the Christian lives, people drink in sin as if it is water. Perhaps they spend their time watching pornographic materials or seedy movies on television. The soul of God's child says, "Away with this! The God I have come to know is most blessed and most holy. He cannot be pleased with this." This consciousness makes a true child of God shun evil and instead love, fear, trust in, and obey God. It is this reality that makes a Christian worship God and really hunger after Him. The eye of faith has beheld Him who is invisible. Consequently, the Christian desires fellowship with God above all else and to be brought more and more into conformity to His image. Only this can satisfy him. Only this brings him deep joy.

This is what makes Christian young adults go into missions work to faraway lands despite seeing their friends make their way up their career ladders. They are willing to give up the comforts that would have been theirs had they continued in their career path, and they do so joyfully with a true sense of fulfillment. Their goal is not to engrave their names in church history among the heroes of the faith. All they are thinking about is how to please the One whom they have seen with the eye of faith. Thoughts about suffering dwindle into utter insignificance in the light of God's glory. They are motivated by the reality of God. All they want is to be with Him, to win souls for Him, to see broken lives mended and flourish in Christ. The world thinks it is madness, but for them it is the only reasonable thing to do. With the eye of faith, they have beheld God.

This applies beyond those who elect to go into missions. It is what motivates those who serve the Lord while remaining in their careers back home. They serve in their local churches and in their communities. They evangelize their neighbors. They give money sacrificially to the cause of Christ at home and abroad. They seek to lead their families in the ways of God despite the culture around them. They do all these things out of a consciousness of God. It is this godly life that causes the world to sit up and take notice of them. These people are different because they see Him who is invisible.

Such Christians impact the world not because they are pastors but because, in their ordinary daily lives, they become the conduits of God's grace to others. The people around them cannot miss the fact that these individuals live differently because they believe in God. Oftentimes these observers may even be churchgoers. It causes them to question their own religious experience. They realize that for them it has become an empty ritual, while for the person they are looking at it is evidently an inner life that is oozing out of their rich spiritual experience. It is the ever-present consciousness of God that makes the difference. It produces true godliness in the family and in the marketplace.

That is godliness. Its source is the grace of God, on the one hand, and faith, on the other. Our active part is not the grace of God. It is ensuring that our faith is a lively faith. Do not overlook this reality, because brotherly kindness and love will not touch other people's lives if true godliness is missing. What others may mistake for love, God, who sees the heart, will know is mere showmanship. Where godliness is present, there is a spiritual energy that is unstoppable and in due season blesses other people.

CHAPTER 11

The Foundation
of Brotherly Kindness

Giving all diligence, add…to godliness
brotherly kindness.

— 2 PETER 1:5, 7

Earlier we looked at how we add godliness to perseverance. If we liken acquiring these spiritual virtues to climbing a hill, we would say that we have arrived at the top once we've reached godliness. It is the highest quality because we are being like God. In this chapter, we begin to descend that hill. We are asking the question, What flows out of godliness? It is love. Love is what shows God's work in a soul. The nature of love is that it rejoices in being a blessing to other people. This is what Peter has in mind when he exhorts us to add brotherly kindness and love to our godliness.

Brotherly kindness and love can be used interchangeably, but when the Bible distinguishes words in this way, it is deliberate. In this case, when the apostle Peter encourages brotherly kindness he is talking about love among the people of God. He is talking about love for one another. When he speaks about love in general, he is now talking about love that spills out to the rest of the world. The apostle Paul also spoke like that in Galatians 6:9–10: "Let us not grow weary while doing good, for in due season we shall reap if we do not lose heart. Therefore, as we have opportunity, let us do good to all, especially to those who are of the household of faith." We are to show love to all people, but we are also to show a particular and special love toward those who are God's children. We will do as the apostle Peter has done, separating them and dealing with one before we go on to the other.

How Brotherly Kindness Starts

Let us begin by asking, What is brotherly kindness? Thankfully, the Greek phrase behind this English expression is commonly used in naming certain places around the world. It is the Greek word *philadelphia*. Yes, that is the name of a famous city in the United States! It comprises two phrases. The first half of the word is the Greek word *phileo*, which means "love." The second part is the Greek word *adelphos*, which means "brother." When you put the two together, it is love for brothers or brotherly love.

Why should the Bible ever separate brotherly kindness from love? It is because when the Bible speaks of brotherly love, it is used in the context of the family. In this case, it is in terms of the Christian family. It is the household of faith that Paul speaks about in Galatians 6. This is not the kind of love between a husband and his wife or people who simply live in a common environment. It is a love that we have for one another because we were born from the same parents or have grown up together in the context of the family. Our homes are not merely boarding houses where we quickly rush in to escape harsh weather. Real relationships are forged there as we live and grow up together. We share a lot in common. We sympathize with and help one another in the demands and challenges of life. When you go and stay at someone's home, you can distinguish the visitors from the family members because there is a chemistry among the people who belong together.

When someone in the family is unwell, the rest of the family never feels that this is an inconvenience. They never say, "Why is this person always falling sick?" No! The rest of the family shows sympathy and cares for the sick person. They can go on for weeks, maybe even months and years, taking turns to nurse the patient back to health. There is a peculiar love that God gives us because we belong to a family. When death takes place, there is a devastation that is peculiar to them even if the person who has died was not the most adorable and good-natured individual. Even if your last conversation ended in a quarrel, when you hear that your brother or sister has died, there is a sympathy that melts you to tears. You feel a sense of emptiness. That sympathy can be referred to as brotherly kindness or brotherly affection. The New Testament applies this phrase to the Christian church as a love that belongs to the people of God. We are truly a family.

This brotherly affection starts at conversion. The Holy Spirit baptizes us into the body of Christ. It is a very real experience. One of the immediate results of this baptism is that for the first time you become interested in other Christians simply because they are Christians. Before you are converted, you go to church the way in which I go to the post office or jump onto a bus. There is no real interest in the other people who are there unless I know them from somewhere else. I am interested only in what I went there for. If it is a bus ride, I simply want to get to my destination.

That is the way it is among non-Christians. When you become a Christian, you suddenly wake up to the fact that you have a new family in the people of God. That is one reason why your relatives never understand you when half the people you want to invite for your wedding reception are church people. To them, church relationships are like office relationships. Your relatives want your wedding to be full of family members. In a sense, they are right. The difference is that you belong to two families now—the natural family and the spiritual family.

Brotherly kindness starts when the Holy Spirit baptizes you into the body of Christ and initiates a sense of belonging. It is more than the comradeship of a political party. It is more than the comradeship you have in your workplace or at school. God the Holy Spirit makes us family. When we refer to one another as "brother" or "sister," those are not just phrases that we have been told to use or which have become fashionable. Spiritually, we really are brothers and sisters.

That is what we are by the work of the Holy Spirit. He makes us one. That is the reason we need to get baptized and join a church soon after our conversion. By doing so, we place ourselves under spiritual oversight. We also begin to exercise real responsibilities toward our brothers and sisters in the Lord. Our common lives go far beyond the time we spend together at church.

How Brotherly Kindness Grows

As we have already seen, when Peter talks about adding one quality to another, he is not talking about bringing in something new. Rather, he is telling believers to grow in the qualities that they already possess in small measure. Here Peter is saying that believers should supplement their godliness with brotherly affection. He wants them to grow in their love for fellow believers. How does that happen? It is brought about by an increasing consciousness of several spiritual realities.

First, you are conscious that you have a common Father, the God and Father of our Lord Jesus Christ. You also have a common elder brother, who is the Lord Jesus Christ. This gives you a sense of family. You are conscious that our Father who is in heaven cares for you together with your brothers and sisters in Christ. You are also conscious that your elder brother is your Savior. He has rescued you from sin along with your brothers and sisters. So you all rejoice in Him. You esteem Him together and consequently you talk about Him.

Second, we have a common belief and confess a common faith. Out of the entire population of the country of Burkina Faso, only 8 percent are evangelicals. Why should we concern ourselves about them? Why should we want to be identified with our brothers and sisters who are in another country altogether? It is because we have a common belief. We believe that salvation is through Christ alone, by faith alone, by the grace of God alone, and, indeed, for the glory of God alone. We believe that outside that gospel there is no salvation. Individuals who do not believe in the gospel go to hell. That belief influences our lives. We want to see everybody come to the knowledge of our Savior, the Lord Jesus Christ. That gives us a common mission and purpose. We want to join hands and labor together for the salvation of sinners.

Third, we have a common life that drives us. Children who are in the same home do many things together. While some are preparing food, others are washing the utensils, others are cleaning the house, others are managing the vegetable garden, and so on. There is a unity and oneness of purpose that is driving them to do things together. That is how it is with Christians. It is partly what causes them to live in love for one another.

Fourth, we have common enemies—Satan, the fallen angels, and the false teachers and slanderers who deliberately undermine the Christian church. We are not indifferent about all these enemies. We are together fighting for the crown rights of King Jesus, our elder brother. We put up a gallant defense against the enemies of God, of the gospel, and of the Christian church.

Fifth, we have common trials. The church is persecuted together. We feel our common woes and so we encourage one another during those trials. We say, "Keep it up, brother. Keep it up, sister. Do not give up. Soldier on!" The sense of family drives us to work together, to live together, and to endure trials together.

Finally, we have common joys. It is more than the joy experienced when a sports team we support wins a game. Our joy is about the triumphs of grace. It is about souls being converted. It is about new churches being planted. It is about new elders coming into the life of the church. It is about seeing marriages mended and backsliders coming back home. Those are the things that thrill us. The people of the world fail to understand this joy we share together, because they are spiritually dead. For us as believers it is real joy, and out of it grows true brotherly kindness.

It is possible, however, to limit this common life and thus deprive yourself of the environment in which brotherly affection grows. For instance, there are true believers who limit their interaction with fellow believers to the time they meet at church. Sadly, they arrive in time for the sermon, and as soon as it concludes, they put on a nice smile as they make their way back to their car—and off they go! They miss out on this rich common life. They do not know who is sitting on their left or on their right in church. They do not know the battles, the trials, the triumphs, and the joys that their fellow believers are experiencing. Brotherly kindness cannot grow in such barren soil. It grows out of the common life of believers as they interact with one another.

Many years ago, when I was in university, we had a student fellowship that we used to call the University Christian Fellowship. It was our habit to greet one another in the first part of our meeting, going from seat to seat, while singing a chorus. I remember the song so well.

> I love you with the love of the Lord,
> Yes, I love you with the love of the Lord;
> I can see in you the glory of the Lord,
> And I love you with the love of the Lord.

What made us want to relate with one another in this unique way was the glory of the Lord in the other person. It gave us a common life on campus as we related to one another. Our lives were connected, and we could sing that song meaningfully.

The more Christlike you are, the more you are drawn to other believers. You want to love them. In other words, the more the Holy Spirit develops in you all those qualities we have been discussing throughout this book, the more you become like Jesus and the more His love flows through you to His people. Jesus wants to love His people. He wants to bless His people, and He does this through you the more Christlike you become.

It is equally true to say that the more Christlike other Christians are, the more you are drawn to loving them. You find that the people of God who come across to you as possessing more of the qualities of Christ tend to draw a certain sympathy out of you. As they show Christ's meekness and love, they draw love out of you. You want to be a blessing to them. Thus, brotherly kindness is mutually edifying and reinforcing. The more Christlike people are, the more you want to love them; the more Christlike you are, the more they want to love you back.

Some individuals complain that there is no love in the church. But if you were to ask them which funeral they last attended in the church, they will tell you they cannot remember. If you asked them which church member they last visited when that person was sick, they will say they wanted to but were very busy. If you ask them which young people they have helped who have needed school fees or transportation money, they will say they did not know there were young people in the church who needed such help. If they had known, they would have helped. That already tells you why the person is not experiencing brotherly affection. What goes around comes around. If you do not care about others, do not be surprised when you fail to experience their love as well. Those who pour out their lives for others are the ones who cause a near stampede when some disaster falls on them. The church rushes to their aid.

Brotherly kindness is spiritual in nature. You cannot engineer it. You cannot hit people on the head every Sunday and say, "You must love one another." You cannot do that and expect that love will flow. In fact, that approach only hardens people's hearts. Brotherly affection grows out of spiritual maturity. The godlier you are, the more you are interested in other people. The more you say, "I've seen that person coming to church lately. Let me find out who they are," the more you will find brotherly bonds growing between you and others.

Finally, brotherly affection grows out of serving together. When you join a church and begin to serve with others in some area of ministry, you will find that the people you are serving with are the ones you develop the deepest bonds with. Initially, everybody is a stranger to you. But as you throw yourself into the work of the Lord, they begin to see your love for their Savior. They get to know you. You are no longer just a face to them. You are a real person who loves the Lord. They can sense the energy and zeal. Then one day they notice you are not there among them. They will call you up and ask if all is well with you. Once you tell them you are unwell or feeling depressed about something, be sure they will be at your door before you can count to ten. Brotherly love grows out of this reality. It is spiritual in nature. This is why it follows faith, virtue, knowledge, self-control, perseverance, and godliness. All of that pours into love for one another.

What Brotherly Kindness Looks Like

Although brotherly affection is in the heart, it reveals itself in action: You esteem your brothers and sisters in Christ. You recognize the glory of your God in them. You delight in them. They are your joy. You empathize with them. What they are going through affects you. You want to do something for them. That is how brotherly kindness looks.

Therefore, you will do everything to maintain fellowship through bearing with and forgiving one another. Colossians 3:12–15 reads, "Therefore, as the elect of God, holy and beloved, put on tender mercies, kindness, humility, meekness, longsuffering; bearing with one another, and forgiving one another, if anyone has a complaint against another; even as Christ forgave you, so you also must do. But above all these things put on love, which is the bond of perfection. And let the peace of God rule in your hearts, to which also you were called in one body; and be thankful." This sense of belonging makes you willing to overlook so much that is done against you as an individual, because you realize that the Christian church is not perfect. We are all sinners who are still being sanctified by Christ. Consequently, you bear with one another. You also genuinely forgive what is done against you because you recognize that we are family.

You will never find a perfect church. Individuals who are always hopping from church to church because someone was gossiping about them in their previous church never grow spiritually. Wherever you go, you will find sinners. People sometimes jokingly say, "If you ever find a perfect church, do not join it, because you will spoil it." Brotherly kindness makes us overlook wrongs, even when people do not acknowledge what they've done against us. We forget about it and move on because we know there is work to do for King Jesus.

When they come to ask for pardon for what they have done, you forgive and go on to work together.

It is brotherly affection that primarily makes you want to help people. We see this in Hebrews 13:1–3: "Let brotherly love continue. Do not forget to entertain strangers, for by so doing some have unwittingly entertained angels. Remember the prisoners as if chained with them—those who are mistreated—since you yourselves are in the body also." Hospitality is not in words only. It is about a room in your home or food on your table. It costs something. It says to people you do not know, "I care for you." Even while you are still a stranger to them, brotherly affection causes you to want to be a blessing. It also causes you to empathize with them. You put yourself in their shoes, so to speak, and allow that to guide your actions. Your own life comes to a standstill because you are empathizing with the brethren in their trouble. Your own calendar changes because of this. Love oozes out of you. As Romans 12:15 puts it, "Rejoice with those who rejoice, and weep with those who weep." Empathy is not always negative. It is also positive. When the brethren have had triumphs, you join with them in their triumphs as though it is your triumph as well. That is what it looks like to share a common life.

In the next chapter we will continue to see what brotherly kindness looks like. For now, let me conclude with this point. There is a major problem with a church where the deacons are the ones doing everything to care for the needy and everyone else is too busy to help. That is not New Testament Christianity. Our faith makes us family, and there is a lot of common life that takes place among us. Remember the words of our Lord Jesus Christ in Matthew 25:40: "Assuredly, I say to you, inasmuch as you did it to one of the least of these My brethren, you did it to Me."

Are you growing in brotherly kindness? It is easy to hide behind others in the church, but before God you are not hidden. He knows what is happening in your life. He knows your self-centeredness. He knows your lack of concern and affection toward His suffering children. If you are totally lacking in brotherly affection toward fellow believers, it could be because He has never saved you. You are merely religious; your name has been added to your church's membership list, but spiritually you are still dead.

I have shown you where brotherly affection comes from. God produces it in your heart when He saves you. His Spirit baptizes you into the body of Christ. You begin to have a sense of belonging to the people of God. They become special to you. If you have noticed that fruit in your heart and it drives you into acts of benevolence toward God's children, then praise God, because it is proof that He has saved you from sin.

CHAPTER 12

Additional Expressions of Brotherly Kindness

*Giving all diligence, add…to godliness
brotherly kindness.*
— 2 PETER 1:5, 7

In the last chapter we had a glimpse of what brotherly kindness looks like. We saw that it includes a readiness to overlook the wrongs that are being done to us, for the sake of the fellowship we have in Christ. There is also a readiness to forgive if the offender comes to ask for forgiveness. Added to this is a deliberate effort to help brothers and sisters when they are in need. We concluded with the empathy that is found in brotherly affection. You weep with those who weep and rejoice with those who rejoice. In this chapter, I want to add three more ways that brotherly kindness manifests itself.

How Brotherly Kindness Expresses Itself

Brotherly kindness makes you use whatever you have to bless other saints to God's glory. You will not simply say, "Depart in peace, be warmed and filled" (James 2:16). You will go to your home or bank to get what your brother or sister needs. You will do all you can to secure the joy of your fellow saints. In 1 Peter 4:8–10, Peter puts it this way, "And above all things have fervent love for one another, for 'love will cover a multitude of sins.' Be hospitable to one another without grumbling. As each one has received a gift, minister it to one another, as good stewards of the manifold grace of God." Notice how he says, "As each one has received a gift, minister it to one another" (v. 10). Use whatever it is that the Lord has blessed you with. That is brotherly affection. The apostle John also adds his own words to this when he says, "But whoever has this world's goods, and sees his brother in need, and shuts up his heart from him, how does the love of God abide in him?" (1 John 3:17).

Brotherly kindness sometimes demands that you make sacrifices in practical ways for the good of other saints. You will go beyond what you can spare and will dig even deeper. That is what Jesus did for us. He sacrificed when He laid down His life for us. He went to the cross and died in our place. First John 3:16 says, "By this we know love, because He laid down His life for us. And we also ought to lay down our lives for the brethren." The Bible is saying that we must also lay down our lives for the brothers. It may not necessarily be in terms of dying, but there is no doubt that it means sacrificing for others.

Brotherly love was evident in the early church. We are told in Acts 2:44–45 that "all who believed were together, and had all things in common, and sold their possessions and goods, and divided them among all, as anyone had need." Look also at Acts 4:32–37:

> Now the multitude of those who believed were of one heart and one soul; neither did anyone say that any of the things he possessed was his own, but they had all things in common. And with great power the apostles gave witness to the resurrection of the Lord Jesus. And great grace was upon them all. Nor was there anyone among them who lacked; for all who were possessors of lands or houses sold them, and brought the proceeds of the things that were sold, and laid them at the apostles' feet; and they distributed to each as anyone had need.
>
> And Joses, who was also named Barnabas…having land, sold it, and brought the money and laid it at the apostles' feet.

Notice how they were selling their property to look after those who were poorer among them. That is sacrifice. The funds were often going to individuals whom they did not even know. They simply sold their possessions and brought the funds to the church leaders, leaving it to them to distribute the proceeds among the needy.

Sometimes the needs of the saints are less tangible. Brotherly kindness also expresses itself at an emotional and spiritual level. Needs do not have to be physical to be very real. For instance, what is it that is going to make you accept brothers and sisters who often rub you the wrong way or with whom you do not see eye to eye on some fine points of doctrine? Brotherly affection is what causes you to accept them.

Another way that brotherly kindness expresses itself is in your prayer life. The Bible says to pray for one another. What will turn your church directory into a prayer guide so that you pray even for those in your church membership you do not relate to directly? It is brotherly affection. When you get news of individuals who have died, you remember their spouses and children who are affected. So you pray for the bereaved. You hear news of brothers and sisters who are sick. You pray for them. You think of those who struggle with school fees and consequently are unable to continue their education. You know that you cannot help them financially, but you get on your knees and pray that the Lord might come through for them. You also pray for those who have backslidden. You want the Lord to bring them back into a spiritual walk with Himself.

Brotherly kindness also expresses itself in the ministry of encouragement. The Bible says to encourage and exhort one another. Certain believers are going through difficult spiritual times. They are discouraged. Brotherly affection demands that you go out of your way to visit them in their home. While there, you speak a word of encouragement to them and thus lift their drooping spirits. That is the way life ought to be with us in the family of God.

Increase Your Brotherly Kindness

Remember, this passage is about growing up. What does spiritual growth look like? We are learning that, among other things, it is about adding brotherly kindness to our godliness. But how do you add brotherly affection? There are at least three ways. First, in terms of quantity: we are to give more and more. Second, in terms of intensity: we are to love more fervently. Third, in terms of sincerity: love must be pure. Let us look at each one of these.

First, our growth in brotherly kindness should be seen in the quantity of our self-giving. In 1 Thessalonians 4:9, the apostle Paul says, "Concerning brotherly love you have no need that I should write to you, for you yourselves are taught by God to love one another." Paul takes it for granted that if you are a believer, you have brotherly affection because the Spirit of God put it in you at your conversion. We considered that fact in the last chapter. But now the apostle wants to see this expressed more and more. Are you a Christian? If so, then one thing I can take for granted about you is that you love the brethren. True brotherly love goes beyond the confines of your local church. It spreads out to Christians in other churches. If there is a need there, you are going to do something about it. The Thessalonians were ministering to Christians throughout Macedonia! Paul asked them to stretch themselves even further. That is Christian growth. You are never satisfied with what you are doing for the Lord now. You want to do more in being your brother's keeper.

Second, our growth in brotherly kindness must be evident in our earnestness. First Peter 1:22 reads, "Since you have purified your souls in obeying the truth through the Spirit in sincere love of the brethren, love one another fervently with a pure heart." We also see the same in 1 Peter 4:8, which says, "Above all things have fervent love for one another." This speaks about zeal and fervency. You cannot miss it when somebody really wants to help you. They will not take no for an answer. Some people who offer help are hoping you will turn it down. That is not earnest. Where there is fervent love, people go the extra mile. There is energy in the expression of brotherly affection. If they are visiting the sick, they want to do all they can to help the person who is unwell. Their hearts are in it. When they are praying for the unwell, you know they are not just hurriedly working their way through a shopping list. They put their heart and soul and mind into their prayer. We need to grow in this expression of brotherly love.

Third, our growth in brotherly kindness must be evident in our sincerity. We saw this already in 1 Peter 1:22. In the early stages of our Christian faith, there is such a mixture in our hearts of the good, the bad, and the ugly. When we are helping anybody, often it is because we want other people to know we are helping. Spiritual growth is when we reach the point that whether the world knows or not is immaterial. We want our help to be to the glory of God.

An obvious example of this sincerity is when a beautiful young lady joins a church. Have you noticed how young men in the church can become very helpful to her? They want to help her with rides to church and elsewhere. They are willing to borrow their parents' car to help this young lady get where she is going. Finally, they pop the question about wanting to court her. The moment she turns down their overtures, the brotherly affection tap runs dry. Was that love sincere? I doubt it. Our brotherly love must not be like that. We should be making progress in sincere love, giving attention without any selfish intentions. There should be less and less of our own agenda and more and more of a commitment to the welfare of others.

It Will Matter on Judgment Day

Let us end with the judgment day. Matthew 25:31–40 says,

> When the Son of Man comes in His glory, and all the holy angels with Him, then He will sit on the throne of His glory. All the nations will be gathered before Him, and He will separate them one from another, as a shepherd divides his sheep from the goats. And He will set the sheep on His right hand, but the goats on the left. Then the King will say to those on His right hand, "Come, you blessed of My Father, inherit the kingdom prepared for you from the foundation of the world: for I was hungry and you gave Me food; I was thirsty and you gave Me drink; I was a stranger and you took Me in; I was naked and

you clothed Me; I was sick and you visited Me; I was in prison and you came to Me."

Then the righteous will answer Him, saying, "Lord, when did we see You hungry and feed You, or thirsty and give You drink? When did we see You a stranger and take You in, or naked and clothe You? Or when did we see You sick, or in prison, and come to You?" And the King will answer and say to them, "Assuredly, I say to you, inasmuch as you did it to one of the least of these My brethren, you did it to Me."

Jesus is talking here about the final day of judgment. It is not the way we normally think about how to enter heaven. It almost sounds as if salvation is by works. There is nothing in this passage about being welcomed into heaven because "you receive Jesus Christ as your personal Lord and Savior." Rather, entry into heaven seems to be based on this: you do this for My little ones! Listen to this:

Then He will also say to those on the left hand, "Depart from Me, you cursed, into the everlasting fire prepared for the devil and his angels: for I was hungry and you gave Me no food; I was thirsty and you gave Me no drink; I was a stranger and you did not take Me in, naked and you did not clothe Me, sick and in prison and you did not visit Me."

Then they also will answer Him, saying, "Lord, when did we see You hungry or thirsty or a stranger or naked or sick or in prison, and did not minister to You?" Then He will answer them, saying, "Assuredly, I say to you, inasmuch as you did not do it to one of the least of these, you did not do it to Me." And these will go away into everlasting punishment, but the righteous into eternal life. (Matt. 25:41–46)

If these words had been written by an uninspired person, we would have said it was erroneous because it seems to be teaching salvation by works. But they were written by Matthew, an inspired author and an eyewitness of the one who said those words—Jesus, the very one who will be the judge. On judgment day, you will not be asked if there was a day when you answered the altar call, or repeated the sinner's prayer, or asked to be forgiven, or were baptized correctly, or joined a good church. Rather, Jesus will look for evidence of regeneration. The evidence will be a life of love, especially for the children of God. Those whom Jesus has saved have received love for their other brothers and sisters.

Based on this Scripture, brotherly kindness is a matter of eternal life or death. Look at your life. Look at what you are spending your time, energy, and money on in the midst of a very needy world where your brothers and sisters in Christ need you to pray for them, encourage them, exhort them, and help them materially. Are you so absorbed with yourself and your own pursuits in life that you are guilty of the sin of omission that is described in this passage of Scripture? It could be evidence of a spurious conversion. Where there is genuine salvation there is genuine brotherly affection.

Do not lull your conscience into believing that Jesus Christ has saved you until you see evidence that He has changed your heart from being self-centered to being God-centered. The proof is not your love for the God you cannot see but rather your love for God's children whom you see every day.

CHAPTER 13

Add Love to Brotherly Kindness

Giving all diligence, add…to brotherly kindness love.
—2 PETER 1:5, 7

We now consider the subject of loving those outside the family of faith. This is the last quality that the apostle Peter wants believers to grow in. As we saw previously, the last two qualities that Peter wants God's people to grow in are the same, strictly speaking. Brotherly kindness is love. However, Peter is now widening the circle of the beneficiaries of love from Christian brethren to the rest of the world.

Its Contrast with Brotherly Kindness

Having already spoken about brotherly kindness, we need to understand what Peter has in mind when he speaks about love. In verse 7, he tells us to add "to godliness brotherly kindness, and to brotherly kindness love." We have said that brotherly affection is the Greek word *philadelphia*. The word he uses for love at the end of the sentence is the word *agape*. This is the love that goes beyond those who belong to the household of faith. It is a love that flows to outsiders. *Agape* is a commitment to the welfare of others primarily because of a need on their part. That is what differentiates it from brotherly love, which emphasizes the relationship between the one loving and the one being loved. *Agape* is a love that you express even to your enemies because it is not dependent on your relationship with them. It is a love that primarily sees their need.

One of the ways in which this love has been referred to over time is "the God kind of love." The reason it is referred to in that way is because of a passage such as John 3:16, which says, "For God so loved the world that He gave His only begotten Son, that whoever believes in Him should not perish but have everlasting life." This is the most well-known verse in the Bible. It speaks of a world that is in rebellion and thus deserving of God's wrath. Yet the thrice-holy God who hates sin with perfect hatred proceeds to love this world and give His own Son as an expression of His love. That is how He saves sinners from the wrath that they rightly deserve. Jesus spoke these words to Nicodemus, a typical Jew who would have nothing to do with Gentiles. The Gentiles were idolaters, without God's written law. They were outsiders and would have been referred to as Gentile dogs. That is how the average Jew would have considered them. So when Jesus said that God so loved the world, He was not speaking in terms of everyone without exception but rather everyone without distinction. He was talking in terms of Jews and Gentiles. He was referring to this fallen, adulterous world—a morally filthy world that was full of sin.

That is why John 3:16 goes on to say, "That whoever believes in Him should not perish." Why should they perish? It is because God's wrath should be on them—they deserve His wrath because of their sin. Look at the very last verse of this chapter. John 3:36 reads, "He who believes in the Son has everlasting life; and he who does not believe the Son shall not see life, but the wrath of God abides on him." God's wrath remaining on us makes sense because the world is in rebellion against God. Instead of God so loving the world, we should expect God to hate it. Yet, wonder of wonders, He loves the world! He acts for the welfare and well-being of a fallen world. The world needs to be reconciled to God, and so, out of love, He provides a way for them to come to Him. What is that way? It is a way of great cost and sacrifice on His part. He gives His Son. He who has the capacity to recreate the whole universe and to repopulate it with a completely new humanity does not do that. He instead sends the best of heaven to take the place of the worst on earth.

That is *agape*. It is a word that is used in the New Testament more times than the other word for love we've discussed, *phileo*. In fact, we are urged to imitate *agape* love because as God's children we are indwelt by His Spirit. We are not to think only in terms of loving those who are in the family of God. We must also love those who are outside this family once we see their spiritual and physical needs. That is why Jesus says to us, "Love your enemies, bless those who curse you, do good to those who hate you, and pray for those who spitefully use you and persecute you, that you may be sons of your Father in heaven; for He makes His sun rise on the evil and on the good, and sends rain on the just and on the unjust" (Matt. 5:44–45). He is commanding us to love individuals who hate us. Why should we love them? First, it is because they need our love, and, second, it is because of the Spirit working in us.

What Love Looks like in Practice

Let us observe what this love looks like in practice. This is important if we are to see that it is not primarily about feelings. Look at 1 Corinthians 13. To appreciate this chapter, one must look at the social and spiritual background of the church that the apostle Paul was writing to. The first converts in the church in Corinth came to repentance and faith in Christ through Paul's ministry. God abundantly gifted them with all kinds of spiritual gifts, which were meant to enable them to minister to one another and to the world. However, these gifts, which were largely of an extraordinary nature, left the church almost destroyed due to internal fights and squabbles. Those who were more gifted than others were proudly seeing themselves as being superior. They were quarrelling over their leaders—who was supposed to be the greatest among them. They were suing each other in court over whatever differences they had among themselves. They were fighting each other over their qualms and scruples. These fights spilled over into their love feasts, where they showed no love for one another. Some were eating gluttonously, while others were starving. Some were even getting drunk in the process.

In addressing the church in Corinth, the apostle Paul dealt with each of these issues. When it came to fighting over gifts, he wanted to show them the more excellent way, which is love. This is what we find in 1 Corinthian 13, where he wrote, "Though I speak with the tongues of men and of angels, but have not love, I have become sounding brass or a clanging cymbal. And though I have the gift of prophecy, and understand all mysteries and all knowledge, and though I have all faith, so that I could remove mountains, but have not love, I am nothing. And though I bestow all my goods to feed the poor, and though I give my body to be burned, but have not love, it profits me nothing" (vv. 1–3). He continues with a description of the nature of love. First, he begins with a positive description: "Love suffers long and is kind" (v. 4). Two positive aspects are mentioned. One is its enduring nature, the capacity to carry on peacefully to the very end. You can tell when you have an impatient driver. He fails to endure traffic jams and ends up hurling insults at fellow drivers. But one who endures with a sense of serenity is still peaceful during the many hours spent in the traffic jam. When you finally manage to get home, you will say to yourself, "I know that this person is very patient." Love is also kind. It is sympathetically benevolent. While enduring, it is acting for the good of those who are around them. That is the combination of being long-suffering and kind. It seeks to meet the needs of others despite a rocky relationship.

The next description comes in the negative form: "Love does not envy; love does not parade itself, is not puffed up; does not behave rudely, does not seek its own, is not provoked, thinks no evil; does not rejoice in iniquity" (vv. 4–6). That is quite a long list of negatives. It is not simply through activity alone that we discern love. It is the entire character of the person through whom love is flowing. When the apostle Paul says that love does not envy, he means that love is dead to the material concerns of this world. We envy people when we see them gaining nicer things or higher status and begin to begrudge their success. This same deadness to the world's priorities is what makes a truly loving person refrain from boasting. He does not put any worth in the things he has acquired. What matters to him is the glory of God and the welfare of others. Boasting results when the wealth you've acquired makes you full of yourself and the world bestows its recognition on you. Love is blind and dead to such things.

The apostle Paul mentions another negative. Love "is not puffed up" and "does not behave rudely" (vv. 4–5). Being "puffed up" refers to an arrogant attitude that demeans people and deliberately drags people's names in the mud. Love does not do that. Rather, it is respectful and wants to honor and uphold individuals in terms of their reputation. Where there is love, there is respect and honor. He goes on to say, "[Love] does not seek its own" (v. 5). This simply means that a truly loving person does not say, "Whatever I want is what must happen." Love is not like that. To this description of love Paul adds that love "is not provoked" and "thinks no evil" (v. 5). A truly loving person is not one who carries a chip on his shoulder for those who have criticized him. He lovingly overlooks wrongs that are done to him. When some people correct you, you can tell from the amount of energy being exuded that this is more than just a correction. This is hitting back. It is a form of revenge. There is a Chinese proverb that speaks of killing a fly on someone's head with a ten-pound hammer. It is obvious that whoever does this is not out to kill the fly. He wants to also hurt the person on whom the fly is sitting, most likely out of hatred or revenge.

The apostle Paul continues, "[Love] does not rejoice in iniquity" (v. 6). When someone has done wrong, love is brokenhearted. It does not rejoice when a person deliberately wrongs somebody else, such as twisting truth into falsity. We see this reinforced in the opposite form as we return to positive descriptions of love: "[Love] rejoices in the truth; bears all things, believes all things, hopes all things, endures all things. Love never fails" (vv. 6–8). Love believes that God is positively at work in the world despite what is going on. Thus, love rejoices with the truth. It celebrates wherever the truth prevails and consequently will bear all things that arise out of the triumph of the truth. This is because a truly loving person hopes that in the end all will be well.

God knows what He is doing. Therefore, a godly person believes all things and for the same reason he hopes all things and endures all things. Love is doing all this while in action for the good of those being loved. Remember, it is the very nature of love to be benevolent. Love is ever acting for the good of those who are its objects.

The apostle ends by saying, "Love never fails." That statement is meant to contrast with the things that the Corinthians were fighting over. Paul is mentioning the things the Corinthians were fighting about that would soon be gone—the gifts of prophecy, tongues, and knowledge. That is why he goes on to say, "Love never fails. But whether there are prophecies, they will fail; whether there are tongues, they will cease; whether there is knowledge, it will vanish away" (v. 8). But the one thing that will not disappear is love. In fact, in verse 13 Paul argues for the supremacy of this virtue: "And now abide faith, hope, love, these three; but the greatest of these is love." What he means is that up to the time when Jesus returns, the characteristics of faith, hope, and love will continue. But, he says, of all these the queen is love—*agape*.

I recall that when we were young, our parents used to take us to the agricultural show. I have never forgotten how we used to envy and literally cry when we saw other children passing by with cotton candy. We really used to envy them because the candy was huge and fluffy. Our parents decided to cure us of those envious thoughts by buying the candies for us. Those candies quickly dissolved as soon as we put them in our mouths. Soon we got to the point where even when we saw someone coming with cotton candy, we did not fuss about it, because we knew it would soon disappear. Paul was telling the Corinthians that they should be concentrating on that which never ends. Hang on to what will endure. Faith, hope, and love will last to the end, but of these three, love is what should be prized above all.

That is what *agape* looks like. It is not waiting to be invited to do good. It is the totality of your life. It oozes these features. Those who know you can tell by these attributes that you are truly a loving person.

This Love Is the Fruit of the Holy Spirit

Where does such a love come from? It is a fruit cultivated by the Holy Spirit. In Galatians, the apostle Paul contrasts the fruit of the Spirit with the absence of this fruit. Our lives before Jesus saved us were characterized by bad fruit: "Now the works of the flesh are evident, which are: adultery, fornication, uncleanness, lewdness, idolatry, sorcery, hatred, contentions, jealousies, outbursts of wrath, selfish ambitions, dissensions, heresies, envy, murders, drunkenness, revelries, and the like" (5:19–21). You cannot miss the fact that these characteristics are works of the flesh and have to do with the absence of love for others. They have to do with a self-centered and selfish life. It is more about bringing others down instead of upholding them. It is more about what we can get out of other people than what we can put into their lives. It is about cursing other people instead of being a blessing to them. That is our world. Turn on your television today, buy your newspaper, check your news online, and that is what you will find. That is the old way of life.

The Christian faith is the opposite because of the fruit of the Spirit listed in verses 22–23: "But the fruit of the Spirit is love, joy, peace, longsuffering, kindness, goodness, faithfulness, gentleness, self-control." When we become Christians, the Holy Spirit not only saves us from sin but also takes up residence in our hearts. Yes, He comes to live in us. If you are a Christian, you are not alone. You are inhabited by the Spirit of the living God. He uses your mind, your heart, and your will to fulfill His agenda of loving redemption. That is His agenda when bringing you into contact with the world around you. First, this agenda applies to the immediate context of the family of believers. You genuinely want to be a blessing to other believers because the Spirit of God is energizing you to do so.

If the Holy Spirit resides in you, the energy that flows from you as brotherly kindness will soon pour out onto the people you meet out there in the world. This is the benevolent energy of the Spirit of God. It fashions your person and your character into what we saw in 1 Corinthians 13. If the Holy Spirit is in you, then His fruit will show.

What we have described in this chapter is what we should want to become in an ever-growing way. Notice how when we reached the height of godliness, that attribute began to pour downhill as a major torrent. It first poured down as brotherly affection. But it did not stop there. It continues flowing in terms of love for others who are outside the Christian faith.

If yours is a selfish and self-centered life, it is the biggest proof that you are not yet a Christian. You may have been brought up in a Christian home and may have learned the doctrines of grace. However, if the kind of love I have described above is missing in your life, it is because the Holy Spirit does not live within you. Has that change happened in you? Can the people who live in your neighborhood truthfully say that they have got a loving neighbor, one who is patient and kind? Or are they afraid of you because you are so irritable? Do they keep a safe distance from you for fear of incurring your violent wrath, like a volcano spewing out molten lava? Do your neighbors see in you a kind person who suffers with them in their afflictions? They may even be afflictions they have brought on themselves because of their sinful lifestyles. Or do they see in you a person whose first reaction is to fight and to make others suffer?

Wherever we are and whatever stage of life we might be in, we should pray that God would help us become better at loving others. We should be praying that until we finally graduate from this life, we will press on and attain new spiritual heights every day. That should be what we strive for in each of our lives—that our spouse, children, and parents would say that over the years they have seen an ever-increasing change. May they see in us a person who is maturing. May God help each one of us to pray that way, that we might be identified as loving people.

CHAPTER 14

A Life of Love Is Reasonable

Giving all diligence, add…to brotherly kindness love.
— 2 PETER 1:5, 7

In this chapter, we go one step further and consider the intellectual reasons that compel us to add love for all to our brotherly kindness toward fellow believers. Before we plunge into that, let me make one statement: Christianity does not start with reason. It begins with revelation. It begins with God revealing to us who He is, His ways, His laws, and His method of salvation. Therefore, Christianity is a given faith. However, even though Christianity begins with revelation, it is very reasonable. When you begin to understand what God has revealed, it is most satisfying to your logical capacity. That is why you find mature Christians to be individuals who have a growing capacity to reason. They show great wisdom in life. It is because Christianity does not begin with reason that the apostle Paul told the Corinthians, "But we speak the wisdom of God in a mystery, the hidden wisdom which God ordained before the ages for our glory, which none of the rulers of this age knew; for had they known, they would not have crucified the Lord of glory" (1 Cor. 2:7–8). They crucified Jesus because they were reasoning with worldly wisdom. In the end, they thought that sending Him to the cross was an opportunity to get rid of an enemy. They did not know that they were playing into God's hands. It was according to plan. Today, we study the cross and the work of redemption that took place at Calvary and find it the most mentally satisfying and spiritually fulfilling truth. We realize that God was substituting the innocent for the guilty, the righteous for the unrighteous, the living for the dying, that we might have a full and free salvation.

We can apply this sense of logic to love as well. God has revealed in Scripture that we ought to add love to brotherly kindness. It is very reasonable that a human being who lives such a life of love finds great fulfillment. Here are at least three reasons why it is the most reasonable thing to do.

God Has Commanded Us to Do So

First, we are to love our non-Christian neighbors because God has commanded us to do so. God commanded it, and therefore we ought to do it. We see this from the way in which the Lord Jesus Christ answered the Pharisees in Matthew 22:34–40:

> But when the Pharisees heard that He had silenced the Sadducees, they gathered together. Then one of them, a lawyer, asked Him a question, testing Him, and saying, "Teacher, which is the great commandment in the law?"
>
> Jesus said to him, "'You shall love the LORD your God with all your heart, with all your soul, and with all your mind.' This is the first and great commandment. And the second is like it: 'You shall love your neighbor as yourself.' On these two commandments hang all the Law and the Prophets."

Jesus was not content with the first and great commandment, although that was enough to answer the question asked. He knew that true obedience to God needs to be both vertical and horizontal. That is, obedience to God is complete only when you love Him and love your neighbor. If all you do is love God, then you are not completely obeying Him. It must be both. Notice the way Jesus summarizes it in verse 40: "On these two commandments hang all the Law and the Prophets." These two commandments are like two plates onto which you can place all the commandments taught in the whole Bible, including each of the Ten Commandments. There will not be a single commandment that does not fit onto either of those plates. So if I am loving God and seeking Him with all my mind, heart, soul, and strength, and I am loving my neighbor as I love myself, I am obeying God.

Usually when international friends are coming to visit Zambia and I am giving them some survival tips, I teach them two very important words. One is in Bemba and the other is in Nyanja. I tell them that those two words will open almost every social door they have to go through. The Bemba word is *emukwai* (which means, "yes, sir" or "yes, madam") and the Nyanja word is *zikomo* (which means, "thank you, sir" or "thank you, madam"). In almost every situation, you can get away by answering with one of those words. Even if you do not know what people are saying, or you are being welcomed into their home, or you are being asked if they can bring you some refreshment, or you are about to leave and they are seeing you off, just keep saying one of those words. They work even when you are trying to make your way through a crowd. So I tell them to keep those two words in their survival kits. They will get them through difficult situations. When it comes to Christianity, the two phrases you can hang on to are "Love God" and "Love your neighbor." These sum up your survival kit.

Love for your neighbor fulfills the second part of the Ten Commandments, which says you shall honor your parents, you shall not commit murder, you shall not commit adultery, you shall not steal, you shall not bear false testimony against your neighbor, and you shall not covet. It is because you love them that you want to avoid hurting them in a physical or spiritual way. You will not want to hurt their sexuality, their marriage, or their family. You will not want to hurt them by taking or destroying their property. You will not want to hurt them in terms of their reputation. By loving them, you are already obeying each one of those commandments.

Although most of these commandments are written in the negative, love enables you to view them positively. Love is what will stop you from simply being content with not harming anybody. Love will make you want to protect your neighbor's life, marriage, family, property, and reputation. Love enables you to joyfully obey God's command. Love takes you beyond the immediate context of church members and causes you to want to be a blessing to whomever the Lord brings in your path. That is the first reason we love our non-Christian neighbors. It is because the Lord God has commanded us to do so, and it is a fulfillment of all His commands about our relationship with fellow human beings. The apostle Paul summarizes this very well for us: "Owe no one anything except to love one another, for he who loves another has fulfilled the law. For the commandments, 'You shall not commit adultery,' 'You shall not murder,' 'You shall not steal,' 'You shall not bear false witness,' 'You shall not covet,' and if there is any other commandment, are all summed up in this saying, namely, 'You shall love your neighbor as yourself.' Love does no harm to a neighbor; therefore love is the fulfillment of the law" (Rom. 13:8–10).

We Have a Lot in Common with Them

Second, we are to love our non-Christian neighbors because we have a lot in common with them. The most obvious commonality is that we are all made in God's image. That is why we show empathy for one another. We are of the same stock, not only in terms of Adam and Eve as our first parents but also in terms of God Himself. He has imbued us with His image.

We also are under a shared condemnation. God said to Adam, "You shall surely die" (see Gen. 2:15–17). That was not only for Adam but for all human beings. All of us are under that condemnation. We all experience disease and death. Therefore, because we are in this together, we must seek to help others who are suffering with us, especially those who are suffering worse than we are. Imagine, for instance, if you had been one of the men and women captured in the heart of Africa and were made to walk to the coast in chains. If you were all given a little soup along the way to drink and then your neighbor on that same chain spilled his as he tried to drink it, would you not want to share your little soup with him? There is a feeling that you are in this together. You need each other. You think that by sharing what little you have, perhaps it might enable both of you to go the full journey to the coast and across the ocean. That is the way it is in life. You find that individuals who are together in prison—whether they are there for crime or as prisoners of conscience or war—develop a comradeship. They are suffering together and, consequently, help one another. We live in a world of injustices. Individuals lose their employment, are fired from their jobs, and are abused in different ways by those in power. Because you have been there, you feel for them and want to do something for them.

What moves us to help others is not only that we have a common condemnation but that, amid that common condemnation, we have a better lot. My companion has spilled his soup, but I still have a bowlful. They are sick, but we are well. They do not have money for school fees, but we have money in the bank. Since I am advantaged compared to them at this time, my heart goes out to them, and I seek to do what I can for them. Have you ever watched a movie depicting a sinking ship where rescuers with smaller boats arrive to rescue people? Have you noticed how those who are rescued almost inevitably turn around to hold the hands of the persons immediately behind them? They were relating to other people on that ship while all was well, and therefore their hearts sympathize with them in their plight. They want to help as many of the other individuals out of that sinking ship as they can before it finally sinks.

There is also the realization that individuals who are in a worse situation have the same potential in life that we have. We want to give them the chance to achieve their potential. This is especially the case with babies, children, and youths who are in desperate need of an adult to look after them. You remember that you were once a child who did not know your left from your right, and you could have easily been destroyed in this hostile and sinful world. You could have easily fallen into the hands of criminals. You were once a teenager whose hormones were running riot, and you would have fallen into anyone's arms who promised you love. Someone older than you helped you to reach maturity safely. Now that you are older, you are not going to turn a blind eye on those youths who need an adult like you to keep a watchful eye over their well-being. You will not be self-ishly content with your marriage, family, finances, and property. You will do what you can for orphaned children so that they, too, may have the opportunity that you had. You want to love the youths you see, whether they are on the streets or in college. You want to be an elder brother or sister who helps them cross over the difficult teen-age years. You want to buy them a book on sexual purity so that they might be armed against the vultures who surround them. You were once in their shoes and know that many of your peers died along the way because they lacked an adult to care for them and to bring them to where you are. You will not be negligent. They have the same potential you had, and you want them to make the most of it.

This is also partly what motivates us to evangelize sinners. It is because we were once there. Our hearts go out to them as we see them embracing prostitutes, staggering out of bars, or getting into trouble in the workplace due to sinful habits. We remember that we were once there until somebody cared sufficiently and reached out to us. We want to do the same for others.

All Kinds of Human Beings Are Needy

Third, we are to love our non-Christian neighbors because all human beings need to be loved, whether they are good or bad. It is not only babies, children, and teens who need loving. We all need the love and care of others. Therefore, we should love all human beings indis-criminately. In a sense, it is easier to love fellow believers and those who have good manners. Sometimes we may wish they were the only ones we were called to love. But loving in this way is like simply paying back a debt we owe. They have been good to us and so we feel like loving them back. Our greatest difficulty is loving someone who has harmed us, someone who is a sworn enemy to us, or someone who wants our downfall in the workplace or at school. That is where we have a real problem. The challenge is to love individuals who hate other people, such as those who are in terrorist organizations. Yet we must pray for them, that God might open their eyes and save them. We must seek to do good to them instead of seeking retribution.

That is where things become difficult. Jesus dealt with this question in the parable of the good Samaritan in Luke 10:

> A certain man went down from Jerusalem to Jericho, and fell among thieves, who stripped him of his clothing, wounded him, and departed, leaving him half dead. Now by chance a certain priest came down that road. And when he saw him, he passed by on the other side. Likewise a Levite, when he arrived at the place, came and looked, and passed by on the other side. But a certain Samaritan, as he journeyed, came where he was. And when he saw him, he had compassion. So he went to him and bandaged his wounds, pouring on oil and wine; and he set him on his own animal, brought him to an inn, and took care of him. On the next day, when he departed, he took out two denarii, gave them to the innkeeper, and said to him, "Take care of him; and whatever more you spend, when I come again, I will repay you." (vv. 30–35)

Our Lord gave this parable when a lawyer was trying to get out of a tricky situation. Jesus had told him to love his neighbor as himself in order to obtain eternal life. In trying to justify himself, this lawyer asked, "Who is my neighbor?" The plot was powerfully woven together by our Lord. Jericho was the city where priests and Levites lived, while Jerusalem was where they worked in the temple. Thus, they would have been rushing to or from work when they came across this man who was bleeding by the roadside. They would have had a good excuse not to attend to this dying man and would've rationalized that someone else would come and handle this. After all, they were either rushing to do God's work or were exhausted from serving Him. They failed to make the connection that we cannot say we love God whom we do not see if we fail to love our neighbor whom we can see (1 John 4:20). Somehow in that moment, there was a disconnect and they bypassed a human being, made in the image of God, in a mad rush to go and prepare the place for worship. Most likely, as we shall go on to see, the person was a Jew. They treated their kinsman in this way with hardly any sympathy. Let us not be too quick to judge them, because we are much the same every day—ever in a hurry! Guess who came after them? It was a Samaritan. Samaritans were like tribal cousins. They were in natural competition and rivalry with the Jews. Jesus deliberately brought this individual into the story because, from a natural standpoint, he would have been the last person to help. Yet Jesus said the Samaritan had compassion on this man. He went over to him and performed first aid before taking him to an inn for further care. He paid his entire bill before recommencing his journey, promising to come and meet any outstanding bills afterward. I am sure the lawyer may have been thinking, *Wow, this must be a rare Samaritan!*

Jesus then asks the lawyer, "So which of these three do you think was neighbor to him who fell among the thieves?" The lawyer answered, "He who showed mercy on him." And Jesus said to him, "Go and do likewise" (Luke 10:36–37). Jesus is saying that when God in His providence brings us into contact with needy individuals, we become their neighbors who should be moved with compassion to do what we can to help them. Putting it another way, when you do something for someone who is needy, you are being a neighbor. Being a neighbor has little to do with living next door or being closely related or being of the same tribe. It is the fact that God has brought you into contact with each other. Remember, the last person to have helped this person was a Samaritan. The Samaritan completely put aside the enmity between their peoples because there was one person who was in need. It was not primarily about his relationship with the stranger. It was about the person's needs, and therefore he did something about it.

Jesus often dealt with this resistance to loving those outside our immediate circle of family and friends, especially those who hate us. To Him, those who overcame this resistance proved that they were regenerate. In His famous Sermon on the Mount, He said,

You have heard that it was said, "You shall love your neighbor and hate your enemy." But I say to you, love your enemies, bless those who curse you, do good to those who hate you, and pray for those who spitefully use you and persecute you, that you may be sons of your Father in heaven; for He makes His sun rise on the evil and on the good, and sends rain on the just and on the unjust. For if you love those who love you, what reward have you? Do not even the tax collectors do the same? And if you greet your brethren only, what do you do more than others? Do not even the tax collectors do so? Therefore you shall be perfect, just as your Father in heaven is perfect. (Matt. 5:43–48)

We are to love all human beings indiscriminately, whether they love us or hate us. That is the reason love is sometimes described in words that suggest the objects of that love are not lovable. First Corinthians 13:4–7 refers to love as being patient, not irritable, not resentful, bearing all things, and enduring all things. It suggests that you need to love people who rub you the wrong way. You must not have the attitude that you will shut the door on them until they have learned to treat you better. No. True love bears all things, endures all things, and never ends. It does not get snuffed out.

This is the love that Peter is referring to in 2 Peter 1:7 when he says, "[Add] to brotherly kindness love." Are you doing this? Are you praying to God, saying, *Lord, help me to do some deed of kindness today, to show Your love to this needy world. May some individuals who are behind me in Your rescue operation feel my helping hand reaching out to them and pulling them forward. Lord, give me a heart like Yours. Make me like You.* This is what Christian growth looks like. Let your life count by living a life of love. It is reasonable because the true purpose for life is loving God and loving others. May the Lord help you to live such a life through Christ to His own glory.

PART 3

The Implications of Spiritual Growth

CHAPTER 15

Possessing and Growing in Spiritual Qualities

For if these things are yours and abound, you will be neither barren nor unfruitful in the knowledge of our Lord Jesus Christ.
—2 PETER 1:8

Sadly, when one looks at what many Christians today are focusing on, you will see that they are all physical pursuits. When you inquire what they are investing in their spiritual growth, you find very little effort on their part. No wonder we fail to have an impact in these days of great trials and sufferings. It is primarily because we are not giving our all to become like Christ. When we come to verse 8 of our passage, we see why we should pursue these spiritual qualities: "You will be neither barren nor unfruitful in the knowledge of our Lord Jesus Christ." That is the incentive. We need to possess and grow in these qualities for our lives to be truly impactful.

Possessing These Qualities Is Assumed

Verse 8 assumes that every healthy believer possesses the qualities we've been discussing over the course of this book. "For if these things are yours…" The *if* used here is not an assumption; rather, it is the basis of an argument. Peter is saying that if you have these things, then this is what will inevitably follow. He is assuming that every true believer will demonstrate virtue, knowledge, perseverance, and so on. If you claim to be a Christian, check to see if you have them in some measure.

The apostle is speaking of us owning and possessing these qualities rather than treating them as a passing phase. Peter speaks of ownership like that of owning land or other durable property. In many African towns, you will see individuals cycling in from the outlying rural areas in the early hours of the morning. They often have baskets or sacks of vegetables on those bicycles. As soon as they arrive in the market squares, they exchange them for cash and head back again. They were in possession of the vegetables for a very short time and are glad to be dispensed with them in exchange for money. That kind of transient possession is not what Peter is referring to. He has in mind a permanent possession. Anybody can think they are Christians when all is well, when everybody is being good to them and there are no temptations or trials to rock the boat of their lives. But the Spirit's work is not transient. It is permanent and deep. That is why the Bible assumes that these qualities are true of every believer. If these attributes are fleeting in your life, then you must go to Christ and ask Him to fill you with His grace and give you the spiritual stamina that can come only from Him.

Growth in These Qualities Is Assumed

The Bible makes it clear that healthy Christians grow in these qualities. Our text says, "For if these things are yours and abound…" Peter's chief concern here is not the possession of these qualities but their growth. This is what the adding is all about in verses 5–7. The actual Greek word that the apostle uses, which is translated as "increasing," is more bountiful than the English word. It has the idea of abundance. The best way to translate it is, "If these qualities are yours and are increasing plentifully." The growth should be so profuse that anyone can see that you are different spiritually and socially. A good example of this is the virtuous woman of Proverbs 31. Her husband says to her, "Many daughters have done well, but you excel them all" (v. 29). Her qualities stand out abundantly.

You are to grow so abundantly in each of these qualities that they are plainly evident to those around you. For instance, in response to your growing knowledge, your fellow believers may begin to suspect that you are becoming quite the biblical scholar. Yet all you desire is to know your God more through the study of His Word. You are never satisfied, and your progress in this quest becomes noticeable.

Peter uses the present continuous tense in this text. He says, "For if these things are yours and abound…" The increasing must never come to an end, because we never arrive at cruising altitude. Before an airplane takes off, the pilot turns on the seat belt sign that prohibits movement on board. The sign remains on until the plane has leveled off at the appropriate altitude. When it is turned off, you can begin to move around and the air crew begins to serve you with beverages. Once you've reached cruising altitude, there is no need to keep climbing higher. The Christian faith is not like that. There is no cruising altitude. We are to be ever climbing and ever growing. This is because we are striving to emulate Christ, who is infinitely glorious. Anyone who thinks he has reached the highest levels of spiritual attainment is merely following idols and not the true God.

These Qualities Are the Fountain of Fruitfulness

These qualities are the fountain of fruitfulness in the Christian life. Look at our text again. "For if these things are yours and abound, you will be neither barren nor unfruitful in the knowledge of our Lord Jesus Christ." These are two negatives that make a positive statement. In effect, then, what Peter is saying is this: "For if these things are yours and abound, they make you effective and fruitful in the knowledge of our Lord Jesus Christ."

If we long to be like Christ, we will be effective in our lives. If we aim directly at being fruitful, we will soon run out of energy and fail. Some church leaders, out of genuine concern for the lukewarmness of their members, invite "revival" preachers to come and stir their members into action. The preachers come with sermons that can melt a rock and set an ocean on fire. Sure enough, for a few weeks and even months after that, there is some extra life in the church. However, it is not long before lukewarmness returns in the life of the congregation. The church leaders make plans to invite other "revival" preachers to stir the congregation back to life. The error is in thinking that effectiveness and fruitfulness can be produced by focusing directly on these outcomes.

It is like weight loss. You do not lose weight by attacking the fat directly. You do it by eating fewer calories and expending more calories. As you do so, your body begins to use its stored fat. Before long people notice that you are becoming slimmer. It is the same in the spiritual realm. Concentrate on growing up and adding the qualities that Peter lists, and the result will be a life that is truly effective and fruitful.

The world desperately needs Christians who are not engrossed in self-preservation and self-aggrandizement. It needs believers who are effective and fruitful amid all the pressures of life. The world hungers for followers of Christ who are overflowing with brotherly kindness and love. The church will answer that longing only when it is filled with believers who not only possess but are growing in the qualities that Peter speaks about here.

CHAPTER 16

The Ineffective and Unfruitful Christian Life

For if these things are yours and abound, you will be neither barren nor unfruitful in the knowledge of our Lord Jesus Christ.
— 2 PETER 1:8

Let us look at the horrible reality and consequences of an ineffective and unfruitful Christian life. One possible explanation for Peter's concern is that he likely witnessed many individuals who professed faith in Christ but were ineffective. Thus, he gave these instructions as a cure for this unprofitable state.

There is nothing more disturbing than being around professing Christians who never produce the fruits of true godliness. They simply flow along, having fun with everybody around them. They do not actively seek to lead other people to faith in Christ. They never purposefully seek to help other believers grow in Christlikeness. Rather, they think that because they have gone to church on Sunday, they have done enough. Peter would have been disturbed by such examples and would have wanted to help professing believers get out of such a rut.

Ineffectiveness

Peter made the point that Christians who prioritize spiritual growth will not be ineffective in their knowledge of the Lord Jesus Christ. The Greek word that is used here is *argos*. It can be translated as "lazy" or "idle" or "useless." It is referring to individuals who are inactive and merely hang around as the day passes by. We have an example of this in Christ's parable about an individual who was hiring people to work in his vineyard. Matthew 20:3–4 reads, "And he went out about the third hour and saw others standing idle in the marketplace, and said to them, 'You also go into the vineyard, and whatever is right I will give you.'" Then verse 6 reads, "And about the eleventh hour he went out and found others standing idle, and said to them, 'Why have you been standing here idle all day?'"

This is very common. Even in our own neighborhood, we see individuals standing on street corners doing nothing. They are completely idle. Some of them can be seen sitting outside homes where the lawn is unkempt. Yet they make no effort to make it more presentable. The word Peter uses represents that kind of lazy situation.

Matthew 12:36 says, "But I say to you that for every idle word men may speak, they will give account of it in the day of judgment." The words they speak are idle words; they do not help anyone. First Timothy 5:13 reads, "Besides they learn to be idle, wandering about from house to house, and not only idle but also gossips and busybodies, saying things which they ought not." This refers to individuals who are occupied with chatter that is merely gossip. They are talking but they are not helping anybody. In Titus 1:12, the apostle Paul says, "One of them, a prophet of their own, said, 'Cretans are always liars, evil beasts, lazy gluttons.'" When the people he is referring to have filled their stomachs with food, all they want is to sit back and engage in lies and gossip. It is the exact opposite of the nature of God. While Jesus was on earth He said, "My Father has been working until now" (John 5:17). God is not an idle God. He created the world and upholds the entire universe. We who belong to Him must be like Him. We must be deliberately effective because people around us are always in need. Some are constantly thinking about death, others are losing their job or are being laid low due to disease. We ought to be busy sharing God's love and ministering to all these needs instead of spreading gossip. Our lives ought to count in the days in which we live. People should attest to how we ministered to them in these very difficult times. If we are growing believers, we will be driven to be effective because the life of God will flow through us like a stream and nourish other people.

Unfruitfulness

Peter also says that if we possess these qualities in increasing measure, they will keep us from being unfruitful in our knowledge of the Lord Jesus Christ. Let us look at what Peter means by being unfruitful. The Greek word that he uses is *akarpos*. It is translated as "unfruitful" or "barren" or "unproductive." It is a phrase we use in agriculture when a fruit tree is barren. It may have good, green leaves, but it has no fruit despite being in the season when other trees are yielding a harvest.

Spiritually, this refers to winning souls to Christ; being fruitful means producing your own kind. For example, a mango tree bears mangoes. Once the seeds in those mangoes are sown, they will produce more mango trees and yield more mangoes. It is the same with human beings. A fruitful womb will bear children who, when they grow up, will also bear children. Human beings are fruitful in producing fellow human beings. Hence, God could say to Adam and Eve, "Be fruitful and multiply" (Gen. 1:28). Produce your own kind through being fruitful. It is the way in which you multiply on the face of the earth. In the same way, Christians produce other Christians through various evangelistic efforts.

This fruitfulness may also mean passing on our godliness to others and building them up in the faith. The work of evangelism leads to the work of edification. Individuals who are saved from sin must proceed to be sanctified. Part of being fruitful as a Christian is when you help others become more and more like Christ through sharing with them the Word of God. You may not be a preacher, but you still want to share what you know with others so that they may grow in godliness. That is what fruitfulness is all about spiritually.

Our fruitfulness in the lives of others is often hindered by our failure to lovingly help people in meeting their felt needs. Let's face it, when we first begin to help people, it is often their physical rather than spiritual needs that we see. It is their need of basic things like school fees, transportation, or medicine. As you help them by sharing your hard-earned resources, they begin to think you are different from so many people around them who are very self-centered. They are amazed that you are helping with no selfish agenda. This opens their hearts and minds to listen to you. This is where you tell them that you are a Christian. The Lord saved you from sin, and He can save them too.

Many Christians mistakenly think that evangelism is all about standing in the open square and simply talking to the first person who walks by. Granted, that is also evangelism, but it is often not as effective as when the example of your life speaks volumes long before you open your mouth. Your faith speaks as you act in brotherly kindness and love. When the stream of affection flowing out of our hearts dries up, it stops us from being productive.

In fact, it is not only the absence of brotherly affection and love but the absence of all the other qualities that Peter has talked about that leaves us ineffective and unfruitful. When you do not possess and are not growing in faith, virtue, knowledge, self-control, perseverance, godliness, brotherly kindness, and love, you will fail to have an impactful life. Let us look at one of these: knowledge. If you are not growing in your knowledge of God, you will inevitably hinder your own effectiveness. If, for instance, you are not growing in your appreciation that your heavenly Father is in sovereign control over everything in your life, this lack of knowledge will leave you full of worry. It will short-circuit your capacity to love others because your energy is being drained through anxiety. I have met believers who have a steady job but who are always trying to ensure that if they lost their job they would not starve or fail to look after their children. Thus, they are busy finding other ways to generate income, in case of that proverbial "rainy day." Although they have enough and some to spare for the poor, they will not give to the needy because they want to prepare for the possibility of losing their income. The

Lord Jesus Christ warned about this in His parable of the sower. He said, "Now he who received seed among the thorns is he who hears the word, and the cares of this world and the deceitfulness of riches choke the word, and he becomes unfruitful" (Matt. 13:22). The Word is unfruitful in their lives, and they end up proving unproductive in the world. When you are not deliberate in studying who God is and what He desires from you, you are robbing yourself of the confidence that can make you very productive.

Fruitlessness is a result of ineffectiveness, which is a result of not being busy about the Lord's work. There are believers who find life boring. How can the Christian's life be boring? How can a farmer's life be boring during harvest season? How can a soldier's life be boring during a war? The apostle Paul ended his letter to Titus with these words: "And let our people also learn to maintain good works, to meet urgent needs, that they may not be unfruitful" (Titus 3:14). He essentially tells Titus to ensure that God's people learn to be committed to good works and to be busy about the Lord's work, helping in urgent cases of need—be it for food, transportation, medicine, accommodation, and so on.

God's Attitude

Why should we as Christians be disturbed about being ineffective and unfruitful? It is because the Bible has given us a preview into eternity. We see God's attitude toward those who claim to be His children and are barren. The reason God has given us this view is to wake us up before it is too late because He does not take kindly to half-heartedness and coldness. Let us see a few examples of this.

As our Lord was drawing to the end of His earthly ministry, He said,

> For the kingdom of heaven is like a man traveling to a far country, who called his own servants and delivered his goods to them. And to one he gave five talents, to another two, and to another one, to each according to his own ability; and immediately he went on a journey. Then he who had received the five

talents went and traded with them, and made another five talents. And likewise he who had received two gained two more also. But he who had received one went and dug in the ground, and hid his lord's money. (Matt. 25:14–18)

The Lord said that the first and second servants were productive and effective. The third was not. The master said to the third servant,

You wicked and lazy servant, you knew that I reap where I have not sown, and gather where I have not scattered seed. So you ought to have deposited my money with the bankers, and at my coming I would have received back my own with interest. So take the talent from him, and give it to him who has ten talents.

For to everyone who has, more will be given, and he will have abundance; but from him who does not have, even what he has will be taken away. And cast the unprofitable servant into the outer darkness. There will be weeping and gnashing of teeth. (Matt. 25:26–30)

That is serious! The Lord was teaching that the unfruitful servant was thrown into hell. How does this fit into the biblical teaching of salvation by grace alone? Often an unproductive soul is a soul that has never really been saved. He or she can be religious but still not saved. True spiritual life bears fruit.

Let us look at another example from the same chapter. We read, "When the Son of Man comes in His glory, and all the holy angels with Him, then He will sit on the throne of His glory. All the nations will be gathered before Him, and He will separate them one from another, as a shepherd divides his sheep from the goats" (Matt. 25:31–32). Let us focus on the goats. Jesus said, "Then He will also say to those on the left hand, 'Depart from Me, you cursed, into the everlasting fire prepared for the devil and his angels'" (v. 41). Why was He sending these people to hell? It is because they were unproductive in a most needy world. Jesus said about those whom He was about to punish, "For I was hungry and you gave Me no food; I was thirsty and you gave Me no drink; I was a stranger and you did not take Me in, naked and you did not clothe Me, sick and in prison and you did not visit Me" (vv. 42–43). In other words, there was no love or brotherly affection in them. The parable ends with the words, "And these will go away into everlasting punishment, but the righteous into eternal life" (v. 46).

If there is a parable that gives me the chills, it is the one the Lord Jesus Christ gave in Luke 13:6–9. In it, the Lord used the story of a barren fig tree to wake us up from spiritual slumber. The passage reads,

> He also spoke this parable: "A certain man had a fig tree planted in his vineyard, and he came seeking fruit on it and found none. Then he said to the keeper of his vineyard, 'Look, for three years I have come seeking fruit on this fig tree and find none. Cut it down; why does it use up the ground?' But he answered and said to him, 'Sir, let it alone this year also, until I dig around it and fertilize it. And if it bears fruit, well. But if not, after that you can cut it down.'"

The vinedresser is asking to aerate the soil around the roots so that perhaps it will cause the tree to bear fruit. At one level you can apply it to Old Testament Israel, which failed to be a light to the Gentiles until it was replaced by the New Testament church. It can also be generally applied to how God deals with those who profess faith in Him. This action can refer to when God brings difficult times in our lives such as sickness, death, or loss of employment to wake us up. Sadly, those who lack true faith go through these situations without being drawn nearer to God and bearing the fruit of salvation. This goes on until God says, "Cut him down! We have wasted enough time on him."

In these parables, Jesus was giving a preview into how God feels about individuals who claim His name but are still warped and self-centered souls who are nothing but ineffective, unproductive, and idle gossips. If the life that Jesus warns about—the life of spiritual idleness—is your life, you are on your way to hell. True faith comes from God, and it never comes alone. It produces good works. You cannot know that God sent His only Son from the glories of heaven into a sin-ridden world, to live a life of poverty and finally die on the cross to bring souls from hell to heaven, and then proceed to live a selfish life. The more you have faith, virtue, knowledge, self-control, perseverance, and godliness, the more you will be filled with brotherly kindness and love, and the more you will be effective and fruitful.

CHAPTER 17

The Blinding Effect of Forgetting God's Grace

For he who lacks these things is shortsighted, even to blindness, and has forgotten that he was cleansed from his old sins.

— 2 PETER 1:9

In light of the benefits that ensue when we make spiritual growth a priority in our lives, one wonders why this goal is not more common among God's children. Why is it that so many Christians prefer to be as close to their former lives of worldliness as possible? This is what the apostle Peter now deals with. He assumes that there are those among the people of God who are lacking in the qualities of spiritual growth and thus are ineffective and unfruitful. He attributes this to their being so shortsighted that they are as good as blind, having forgotten God's grace that brought them to salvation and cleansed them from their former sins. We would say today that they have forgotten God's marvelous and matchless grace. They lose the thrill, the sparkle, and the joy of knowing that God has had mercy on them. Let us look at how Peter opens this up for our own edification.

The Lack of These Qualities

In verse 9 the apostle illustrates what it is like when someone lacks the qualities he has been writing about in verses 5–7. To lack these qualities does not mean that you never manifest them. You may not be totally ignorant of Christianity, but you cannot be described as a knowledgeable Christian. You exhibit some level of self-control and steadfastness, but when it comes to your darling sins, you indulge yourself like someone who has never experienced salvation. From time to time you act to alleviate the suffering of others, but those who are close to you cannot refer to you as a loving person. If this describes you, then Peter is addressing you as one lacking these qualities of true spiritual growth. Perhaps once upon a time you were growing spiritually and your life was having an impact on others. Today, there is very little difference between people who have never been saved from sin and yourself. At the most, perhaps, you can be described as lukewarm. You go to church purely as a habit but certainly not because you are thirsting for more knowledge about God from His Word. You would rather be somewhere else and making money. Thus, you are absent-minded in church and easily distracted. Yet as soon as you are out of church and surrounded by worldly company, you come alive. If you have been a Christian for many years, you even sneer at those who manifest unusual zeal for the Lord Jesus Christ. You say that such a life is not realistic. You are lacking in the qualities of spiritual growth and thus are a very poor representation of true biblical Christianity.

A Result of Spiritual Blindness

Why would anyone be content with that kind of life? Peter says that people who live like this are shortsighted and spiritually blind: "For he who lacks these things is shortsighted, even to blindness, and has forgotten that he was cleansed from his old sins" (2 Peter 1:9). It is amazing how two people can both wear glasses for very different reasons. For one person it is because they cannot see far, and for the other it is because they cannot see objects that are very close to them. My wife, Felistas, is nearsighted and so she takes off her glasses when she is reading. I am always fascinated by this because I am farsighted. I cannot read without my glasses. Everything is blurred. I can drive without my glasses because I see distant objects very well. But my wife cannot drive without her glasses. To her, everything far away is blurred. In our text, Peter is using this phenomenon—people like my wife—to refer to a spiritual reality. He has in mind people who are so conscious of the immediate physical world around them that they fail to see that which is spiritual and eternal. They are overwhelmed with the immediate, with what is in the news today, and that is what has captivated them.

Peter uses a physical example to demonstrate a spiritual reality. He is referring to individuals who are so enamored by the physical things of the world that they no longer function or think along spiritual lines. They are overwhelmed with activities like finishing school, getting a job, getting married, having children, making more money, getting promoted, owning a business, owning property and cars, and so on. That is what excites them or leaves them very anxious. When anything happens in their lives that threatens these pursuits, they become disoriented. When they lose a child or a spouse, they are completely knocked off course. When illness takes away what they were leaning on, they despair. They are unfruitful in such times.

Such people are ineffective both when chasing after the things of this world and when the things of the world are snatched away from them. They have no spiritual stamina to handle such situations. They lack the knowledge of God's sovereignty, and so when you share God's Word with them to give them comfort in their moments of suffering, they are unable to relate to those biblical truths. They feel as if God is unfair and as if He hates them because their agenda has been disturbed by the negative circumstances in their lives. They fail to see that God hides a smiling face behind the dark cloud. They have become blind.

When such people are in church sitting under the preaching of eternal realities, they can hardly identify with anything the minister is saying. They say that church is boring because the subject matter is not about how to be successful in this world. When they hear about sanctification or the way in which God wants us to live a life of obedience and commitment to Him even in the trials of this world, the message goes in through one ear and out through the other without touching their hearts. They feel as if they are in the wrong place. They want to be where they will be told how to be great in this world.

Christianity is about grace and sanctification here below and glory in heaven above. The apostle Paul captured something of this when he wrote, "Therefore we do not lose heart. Even though our outward man is perishing, yet the inward man is being renewed day by day. For our light affliction, which is but for a moment, is working for us a far more exceeding and eternal weight of glory, while we do not look at the things which are seen, but at the things which are not seen. For the things which are seen are temporary, but the things which are not seen are eternal" (2 Cor. 4:16–18). Paul was speaking about Christians who are going through a difficult time, including himself. He said that they were not discouraged or overwhelmed by these difficulties. Outwardly they were wasting away. That was undeniable. Anyone could see that. Yet, because they were not shortsighted, their spiritual eyes saw eternal realities that kept them renewed, refreshed, and growing into maturity because of those very circumstances. Since their eyes were looking beyond the immediate, they saw the trials they were going through as light and momentary.

In case you think that these were light and momentary by worldly standards, Paul has given a sample of what he had in mind:

> Are they ministers of Christ?—I speak as a fool—I am more: in labors more abundant, in stripes above measure, in prisons more frequently, in deaths often. From the Jews five times I received forty stripes minus one. Three times I was beaten with rods; once I was stoned; three times I was shipwrecked; a night and a day I have been in the deep; in journeys often, in perils of waters, in perils of robbers, in perils of my own countrymen, in perils of the Gentiles, in perils in the city, in perils in the wilderness, in perils in the sea, in perils among false brethren; in weariness and toil, in sleeplessness often, in hunger and thirst, in fastings often, in cold and nakedness. (2 Cor. 11:23–27)

Momentary affliction? I know it doesn't sound like it. Paul is speaking in comparison. He sees it as preparing for us "a far more exceeding and eternal weight of glory." His spiritual eyes are not blind or myopic. He is farsighted. He is seeing what will happen because of these afflictions when he gets to the other side. That is the reason Paul could say, "We do not look at the things which are seen, but at the things which are not seen. For the things which are seen are temporary, but the things which are not seen are eternal" (2 Cor. 4:18).

Worldly believers are the exact opposite. They do not see eternal things. So, when they experience afflictions, they easily give up. Why? It is because they are shortsighted to the point of being blind. They see only their immediate suffering. They fail to see what it is achieving for them. Everything they live for is on this side of eternity. When they lose what their hearts crave, they go into a depression. What a pitiful state to be in!

A Result of Forgetting God's Grace

We need to dig deeper. What causes this spiritual blindness? It is when believers forget God's pardoning grace. Peter says, "For he who lacks these things is shortsighted, even to blindness, and has forgotten that he was cleansed from his old sins" (2 Peter 1:9). He is referring to the forgiveness of sin that took place at the point of our conversion when we went from death to life, from darkness to light. We were liberated from being an object of the wrath of God and from the threefold enslavement that unbelievers labor under—enslavement to the devil, the world, and our sinful nature. All believers should be able to look back and say along with hymn writer William Newell,

> Years I spent in vanity and pride,
> Caring not my Lord was crucified,
> Knowing not it was for me He died on Calvary.
>
> By God's word at last my sin I learned—
> Then I trembled at the Law I'd spurned,
> Till my guilty soul imploring turned to Calvary.

> Mercy there was great and grace was free,
> Pardon there was multiplied to me,
> There my burdened soul found liberty—at Calvary.[1]

Calvary was the place where our pardon was purchased. We sinned and deserved to go to hell. God's wrath was hanging over our heads. Yet the same offended God took His Son—the best of heaven—and sent Him here on earth to suffer and finally die on the cross. He suffered the most excruciating form of punishment that existed at that time. The wrath of the sin-hating God was poured on Jesus to its very dregs until He cried out, "My God, My God, why have You forsaken Me?" (Matt. 27:46). It was for the sake of sinners that Jesus remained hanging there. He was paying the price for sin so that salvation may be free for all who repent and trust in Him. It is this free salvation that is unforgettable.

If you are a Christian, you know what Newell was expressing. He was referring to the day he finally said,

> Now I've given to Jesus ev'rything,
> Now I gladly own Him as my King,
> Now my raptured soul can only sing of Calvary.[2]

Do you remember those days when your soul was overwhelmed with the grace of God? The only thing you wanted to do was to tell the whole world that God pardons sinners. That was your food and drink—your everything! Your spiritual eyes were opened, and spiritual things were very real to you. That was why eternal damnation shook you to the core until you sought the Savior. It is the very reason why eternal glory excites you to the point that you say it is worth dying for it. Calvary is what has brought about that difference. It is because God does not want us to forget about His grace poured out for us on Calvary that He instituted the two ordinances—baptism and the Lord's Supper. Both point to the death of the Lord Jesus

---

1. William R. Newell, "At Calvary," Hymnary.org, accessed February 8, 2024, https://hymnary.org/text/years_i_spent_in_vanity_and_pride.
2. Newell, "At Calvary."

Christ on the cross. When instituting the Lord's Supper, Jesus said, "Drink from it, all of you. For this is My blood of the new covenant, which is shed for many for the remission of sins" (Matt. 26:27–28).

God wants our spiritual eyes to always gaze at the cross so that we do not grow weary in this world of temptations and trials. We are to exchange the cross for the crown only when we arrive in glory. As long as the cross remains in our view, we will want to love God in response. He has paid a debt that we never could have paid. The divine, infinite, and matchless grace of God pouring over the soul of a pardoned sinner causes the heart to want to love Him back. The best way to love Him is to be the best for Him. This inspires the striving after knowledge (how best to live for God) and the desire to be self-controlled and steadfast for God's glory. As part of loving God, the pardoned sinner wants to love His people and His world. That is why the apostle Paul writes to Titus about Jesus Christ, "who gave Himself for us, that He might redeem us from every lawless deed and purify for Himself His own special people, zealous for good works" (Titus 2:14). Calvary is the combustion chamber in which the energies of spiritual service are released. It produces people passionate about serving Christ. They are effective. They are fruitful. You cannot miss it.

When believers forget the cross, they lose their first love and become lukewarm. They no longer think about the great transaction that took place when the Lord saved them. They forget the price that was paid to bring them into God's family. They no longer remember what it meant to take off their stinking grave clothes and put on the righteousness of Christ with its heavenly aroma. They begin to take their Christian life for granted.

CHAPTER 18

Confirm Your Calling
and Election

Therefore, brethren, be even more diligent to make your call and election sure, for if you do these things you will never stumble.
— 2 PETER 1:10

Having seen what happens to us when we do not make our own spiritual growth a priority, we are now ready to hear the apostle Peter urging us once again to make this growth a vital part of our lives. We have seen that one of the benefits of striving after spiritual growth is that your life becomes productive. You count in God's kingdom. You bear fruit that is evident to all. People praise God for the impact your life is having on theirs. In this chapter we will see that when you do what Peter is telling us all to do, you also gain a stronger assurance of your own salvation. You sense more and more that you are a child of God. Out of this grows a stability in your spiritual life that was not there before.

Confirming Your Calling and Election

The first benefit of seeking spiritual growth is the confirmation of your calling and election. When you are adding these spiritual quali-ties to your life, and are diligent about them, you are at the same time indirectly growing in your assurance. Our English version begins with the word *therefore*, suggesting that what comes next is a result of what he has been speaking about. He says, "Therefore, brethren, be even more diligent." What has he been saying that makes this a

wise conclusion? We saw in verse 8 that as we are adding these qualities to our spiritual lives, we become more effective and fruitful. As
a result of our becoming more productive, we gain a greater sense
of assurance.

At this point, Peter is very absorbed in what he is writing. He
refers to the people he is writing to as "brethren." This is the only
place in his two epistles that he uses this term, so it must be deliberate. The term he is most fond of using is *beloved* (see, for instance,
2 Peter 3:1, 8, 14, 17). It is his favorite word. But now he says "brethren." Peter is making an appeal to all those who claim to be Christians
that they should grow spiritually as a sure way of really knowing that
they are in the Lord.

Peter urges his readers to do so with eagerness. He writes, "Be
even more diligent," as if to say, "Run with all your strength." It is
reemphasizing what he said in verse 5: "giving all diligence." You
must make this your highest priority. Why? Because it is confirming your calling and election. As an apostle of Christ, he knew how
important this was for believers. Confirming your calling and election is not yet another step in adding spiritual qualities to your
life—it is a by-product of this way of life.

I remember when I was growing up, we used to have cousins
coming to stay with us during school holidays. It often added color
to family life. I had one cousin who was as skinny as a broomstick.
It must have been his genetic makeup, because he ate a lot, yet it
did not show on the scale. What I particularly recall was his extra
effort to gain weight. As he would be swallowing his food, he would
be indicating an outward motion with his hands from his stomach
as though to say to it, "Protrude outwardly. I need to grow fat." Of
course, that never happened, because it is the food being eaten that
leads to weight gain and not some motions of the hands. Similarly,
Peter is not asking you to do something more than what he has
already told you to do. All he is saying is that the more you give
yourself to this process of spiritual growth, the more you will con-
firm your calling and election. It will result in you singing,

Blessed assurance, Jesus is mine!
Oh, what a foretaste of glory divine!
Heir of salvation, purchase of God,
Born of his Spirit, washed in his blood.

This is my story, this is my song,
Praising my Savior all the day long.
This is my story, this is my song,
Praising my Savior all the day long.[1]

All this is a result of adding the spiritual qualities to your life. Let us look at virtue as one example to make this point easier to appreciate. We said that it stands for excellence. A virtuous Christian is someone who exhibits the highest levels of godliness. He is never satisfied with mediocrity in his walk with God. What causes a Christian to seek such a life of virtue? It is simply gratitude for the salvation he has come to experience in Christ. God gave the best of heaven for him, and so he wants to give his all for God. This is what makes the difference between a person who is merely religious and one who has experienced salvation in Christ. I recall how in my childhood days our parents would give us offertory money for church. Upon getting to church, we would look for smaller currency coins in our pockets and put those in the offertory basket instead. Our parents would think we were offering the money they gave us, so it saved us from getting into trouble. We wanted to give the least we could give without getting into trouble. That is not the attitude of a true Christian. Upon my conversion, my attitude totally changed. I now respond to God's love for me and want to give to His cause as much as I possibly can without hurting my finances. What has changed? It is the fact that the Lord has saved me. I want to exhibit excellence in supporting God's cause.

---

1. Fanny Crosby, "Blessed Assurance," Hymnary.org, accessed February 8, 2024, https://hymnary.org/text/blessed_assurance_jesus_is_mine.

Before we move on, let us note how the apostle Peter uses the double phrase "call and election." Calling refers to the work that Jesus does by His Spirit at the point of our conversion. It refers to effectual calling, the life-giving call that takes us from death to life, out of the kingdom of darkness and into the kingdom of God's marvelous light. The apostle Paul talks of God's call and the conversion that takes place when individuals become His children in 1 Corinthians 1:24: "But to those who are called, both Jews and Greeks, Christ the power of God and the wisdom of God." He speaks of those who are called through hearing the gospel. Their eyes are opened to understand the good news that saves sinners through the person and work of our Lord Jesus Christ. This results in experiencing the power and wisdom of God. However, behind that call is the electing grace of God the Father. These two go together.

Let us return to Peter's main point. As you pursue the spiritual qualities he has mentioned, you will make your calling and election sure, which should make you all the more eager in striving for spiritual growth. Look around you in the context of your own church. Do you see believers who seem to be enjoying spiritual love, joy, and peace? They seem to be full of God. What is it that has distinguished them from the other believers in your church? I want to suggest to you that it is this very matter that Peter is speaking about here. Those believers have made the matter of their spiritual growth a priority in their lives. They are never content with just going with the flow. They have come to know the Lord and want to know Him more. In their trials, they deliberately want to know more and more of what it means to persevere. They want to be God-centered in all situations. That is why you cannot miss their godliness. They live their lives around the people of God, serving their brothers and sisters. They give their time and money to the well-being of the saints. They want to be a blessing to God's world. Their lives are fruitful as they seek ways to make that desire practical. It is all a result of their spiritual growth. It goes a long way to confirming them in their calling and election.

You Will Not Ultimately Fail

The second benefit is that pursuing spiritual growth keeps you away from falling off the spiritual cliff. It ensures there is ground under your feet. In other words, it gives you stability in your Christian life. In speaking about making your calling and election sure, Peter was dealing with assurance about what has happened in the past. Regarding this second benefit, he is talking about the future. You are assured that you will never fall. Let us read his words again. "Therefore, brethren, be even more diligent to make your call and election sure, for if you do these things you will never stumble" (2 Peter 1:10).

This is slightly different from the phrase "Once saved, always saved." Whereas it is true that once the Lord saves you, you cannot lose your salvation, your assurance of that truth in your personal life is connected with what we are learning here. The weakness of the phrase "once saved, always saved" is the implication that it does not matter how you live. You can be half asleep spiritually and you need not worry; all will still be well. You can fall into sin and live in it; do not worry, you will still make it. That is not what Peter is teaching here. The better phrase is "the final perseverance of the saints." It is better to speak of perseverance because it suggests effort, grit, and resolve. It is crucial that we do not miss that. It's only as you persevere in growing in these qualities that you are confirmed that your faith is genuine and you can be assured you will not fall.

Here Peter is talking about falling into sin in a way that tarnishes your testimony and becomes visible to all. As much as people may want to overlook the situation, they know that this person has messed up badly. When a person is not engrossed with trying to reach the highest point spiritually, he makes himself vulnerable to the Evil One, who makes him terribly prone to unthinkable sins.

Let me go further and suggest that Peter is not only talking about damaging one's testimony. He implies missing heaven altogether. I am making this suggestion based on the next verse: "For so an entrance will be supplied to you abundantly into the everlasting kingdom of our Lord and Savior Jesus Christ" (2 Peter 1:11). Peter is saying that if you are not adding these qualities to your life, it may be a confirmation that you were not called or elected in the first place. The diligent acquisition of these qualities shows that spiritual life is in you. The absence of this fervor proves that you never had spiritual life all along. Thus, when temptation comes, you will fall because there is no solid foundation under you. The structure you were trying to build collapses. You were content to simply follow the crowd in the background while God's true children were making serious progress spiritually.

This is what we often find in the church. Individuals who do not take Peter's counsel seriously soon fall away. Consider the typical example of adults who want to get married but no one in the church is interested in them. Then some unbeliever in their workplace pursues them and they make shipwreck of their lives. They fall away. They belong to the category that Jesus referred to in the parable of the sower. He said, "But he who received the seed on stony places, this is he who hears the word and immediately receives it with joy; yet he has no root in himself, but endures only for a while. For when tribulation or persecution arises because of the word, immediately he stumbles. Now he who received seed among the thorns is he who hears the word, and the cares of this world and the deceitfulness of riches choke the word, and he becomes unfruitful" (Matt. 13:20–22). These people profess faith, but they fall away or prove unfruitful. They are not true Christians.

Such individuals were always content to live very close to the edge of spiritual destruction. Thus, when Satan tempted them, they swallowed his bait and were gone. Such people not only damage their testimony; they also do not go to heaven. The abundant entry will not be theirs. It is important for all of us to look at our lives and ask ourselves the question, Am I saved, or am I not? If we are still living selfish and self-centered lives, we should doubt whether Christ has truly saved us. Our Savior gave His entire life, leaving the throne of heaven to come and die in our place. He suffered as He did on earth and finally took our sins and paid for them on the cross. How can we treat Him and His cause with such disinterest? How can we make marriage or a job or a promotion the most important thing in our lives? Clearly, this simply betrays the fact that we have never had spiritual life, and our well-deserved end is hell.

This is why it is so important for every professing Christian to grow up. Our present spiritual joy depends on it. Our future felicity depends on it. Our very lives depend on it. In growing up, we show that we are true Christians. As the hymn says,

> Deeper, deeper, in the love of Jesus
> Daily let me go;
> Higher, higher in the school of wisdom,
> More of grace to know.
>
> Deeper, deeper! blessed Holy Spirit
> Take me deeper still,
> Till my life is wholly lost in Jesus,
> And His perfect will.
>
> Deeper, deeper! tho' it cost hard trials,
> Deeper let me go!
> Rooted in the holy love of Jesus,
> Let me fruitful grow.
>
> Deeper, higher, ev'ry day in Jesus,
> Till all conflict past,
> Finds me conqu'ror, and in His own image,
> Perfected at last.[2]

This should be our daily cry.

---

2. Charles Price Jones, "Deeper, Deeper," Hymnary.org, accessed February 8, 2024, https://hymnary.org/text/deeper_deeper_in_the_love_of_jesus.

CHAPTER 19

An Abundant Entrance into Heaven

For so an entrance will be supplied to you abundantly into the everlasting kingdom of our Lord and Savior Jesus Christ.

— 2 PETER 1:11

We now come to the final implication of all that Peter has been urging on the believers since the start of this letter. He wants us all to enjoy an abundant entry into heaven. Can there be a better argument to woo us out of a state of indifference toward the whole subject of Christian growth?

In the previous verse, Peter spoke in negative terms when he said, "You will never stumble." He now puts it positively. If you do all that he has been urging you to do, you not only will be kept from falling but will receive a rich welcome into heaven. There are at least three implications from this verse.

This Is the Normal Christian Life

The apostle has just finished outlining the effectiveness, fruitfulness, assurance of salvation, and stability that should be evident in your life (vv. 8–10). If all this is true about you, then what he is about to describe will also be true.

If we go back to verses 5–7, we find the foundation of the imperatives of spiritual growth. This is the backdrop of everything the apostle is saying here. Being effective, assured, and stable in your Christian life does not happen by accident. It is the fruit of a life that is growing in virtue, knowledge, self-control, perseverance, godliness, brotherly kindness, and love. If you are growing in all these, then you will have a rich entrance in heaven.

If we go even further back, we find that the ultimate foundation for all this is what God Himself has done. Divine indicatives give birth to human imperatives. The Christian faith is not a religion built on a foundation of good works. It certainly has good works, but they grow out of what God has done for us and in us. As the apostle Paul put it to the Philippians, it is God who works in you to will and to do according to His good pleasure (2:13). As God works in you, your life become fruitful. We saw earlier in 2 Peter 1 that God has done the following:

- He has given us a faith of equal standing (v. 1).
- He has given us everything else that we need for godliness (v. 3).
- He has also given us His great and glorious promises (v. 4).

Let us now put all this together. The first backdrop Peter has in mind is the indicatives of our Christian faith. It is the foundation of everything. Our spiritual lives depend on what God has done. He has given us the faith, the divine power, and the promises through which we escape this wicked and sinful world. The second backdrop is the imperatives of the Christian faith. God will not do this for us. He commands us to be responsible and to add spiritual qualities to the foundation of what He has done for us and in us. God laid the foundation, and we build the superstructure with His help. This superstructure will make some Christians look like my grandfather's hut, while others look like a skyscraper in Manhattan. The difference is the effort individual Christians put into their spiritual growth. Peter then speaks of the implications of all this. If you prioritize spiritual growth, you will know true effectiveness, fruitfulness, assurance, and a stable spiritual life. That is Christianity!

Before we proceed, we must ask whether Peter's summary is true about us. We claim to be Christians. Is the apostle's description reflected in our own spiritual lives? Sadly, too many people who claim to be Christians cannot be described in this way. As I have stated frequently in this book, they live like every worldly person in the world except they attend church on Sundays. Nothing in their life approximates the spiritual growth Peter describes. Whereas we have accepted such individuals as Christians simply because they claim to be so, Peter warns that such individuals will not get to heaven. What he has been describing is the normal Christian life. It is not the spiritual life of giants in godliness. If the apostle's description of the Christian life does not ring true of your life, throw away whatever it is you are hanging on to and start afresh before it is too late. If you die as you are, you may hear God say on the final day of judgment, "I never knew you; depart from Me" (Matt. 7:23).

The Generous Response of God

The God who laid the foundation and urges us to grow responds to our obedience with gracious generosity. Look at the way Peter puts it in our text: "For so an entrance will be supplied to you abundantly into the everlasting kingdom of our Lord and Savior Jesus Christ." It is the way parents teach a child to walk. They do it with incentives so that the child may finally gather enough courage to walk. As soon as the child walks a few steps, the parents grab the child and clap with loud cheers as if walking those few steps is the greatest achievement in life. But it does not end there. As the child grows older, the parents want their child to have great achievements in school. Again, they make promises: "If you come out as one of the top ten students in your class, then we will buy you that bicycle you have always wanted." What is promised is far greater than coming out among the top ten in the class. The parents want to encourage their child to work hard. Yet when you really examine the situation, you soon realize that it is the parents who do most of the work. They are the ones who house the child, feed the child, pay school fees, buy uniforms, take the child to school, check homework, and so on. Granted, the child must also play a part. It is the child who must write, study, and make the effort. The parents lay the foundation, and the child builds the superstructure.

That is what we see here. God lays the foundation of faith, of divine power, and of His own precious promises. He then encourages us to build the superstructure with His help. We put in the effort, we toil, we labor, and we love. We do whatever is needed. Finally, He responds in generosity. To borrow the words of Paul from 2 Corinthians 9:6, "He who sows sparingly will also reap sparingly, and he who sows bountifully will also reap bountifully." The emphasis of this text is in the word *bountifully*. Can you imagine God pouring His generosity into your life? He owns all things in creation. This is not some poor uncle who gives you a hundred dollars and believes he has richly blessed you. This is God, who owns the entire universe. He is the one who is responding in this rich and glorious way.

The sobering reality is that, according to the Bible, we will live for eternity. How we live in that eternity hangs on God's assessment on the day of judgment. Look at 2 Corinthians 5:9–10, where the apostle Paul says, "We make it our aim, whether present or absent, to be well pleasing to Him." Why? "For we must all appear before the judgment seat of Christ, that each one may receive the things done in the body, according to what he has done, whether good or bad." We live to please God and not to please ourselves, because we have an account to give to Jesus Christ in eternity. Instead of asking, "What is wrong with me listening to this music or dressing this way?" we should be asking, "How can I please the Lord in the music I listen to or in the way I dress or the way I use my time?" In 1 Corinthians 3:12–15 Paul says, "Now if anyone builds on this foundation with gold, silver, precious stones, wood, hay, straw, each one's work will become clear; for the Day will declare it, because it will be revealed by fire; and the fire will test each one's work, of what sort it is. If anyone's work which he has built on it endures, he will receive a reward. If anyone's work is burned, he will suffer loss; but he himself will be saved, yet so as through fire."

The Rich Entrance into Heaven

The Bible refers to our entrance into the kingdom of our Lord and Savior Jesus Christ in different ways. The first way happens at the point of our conversion. When we repent of our sins and believe in Jesus Christ, we enter the kingdom and become its citizens. The second way is when we die and enter glory. The third way refers to the entrance we make after undergoing the final judgment. That will be the permanent eternal state. It seems to me that by adding the word *everlasting* to the word *kingdom*, the apostle Peter has in mind what will happen when Christ Himself returns to judge the world. It is at this point when Jesus will reward His own. It will be preceded by the final resurrection. In our glorified bodies we will be ushered into His eternal kingdom and receive our eternal inheritance and reward. History will have come to an end and everyone who is the elect of God will have been saved. Peter is saying that if we live as he has urged us to, we will receive this abundant entrance into the kingdom. We will hear the words, "Well done, good and faithful servant" (Matt. 25:21).

It is like the extravagance we witness when our national sports team returns home after winning a continental or world competition. I remember this happening when the Zambian national soccer team won the Africa Cup of Nations (AFCON) tournament. That was a richly rewarding return to Zambia! It felt as if the whole nation lined the streets to welcome the heroes back home. Even police could not stop people from standing in places where we are not normally allowed to stand. The noise was electrifying, especially when the soccer players started coming out of the plane carrying their trophy. There was a euphoria as the whole nation cheered. The president of Zambia canceled whatever he had on his schedule for that day to host a banquet for the heroes. Our national broadcasting station canceled its normal programming to capture this event live all the way to State House. The nation poured a fortune into welcoming back these heroes. It was a rich provision. The soccer administrators and players had given their all to win that trophy.

A lot went into the preparations for the tournament. The team spent months in training so they could achieve optimal levels of teamwork, defense, and scoring. When the competition started, the administrators and players put aside everything else in their lives to focus on winning the trophy. Having achieved the goal, the result was this abundant welcome!

I wonder if that is what you look forward to—this bountiful welcome into heaven. Are your eyes set on your entrance into this eternal kingdom? This is what God has promised to give His children who show spiritual maturity and fruitfulness in this life. It is amazing how all this is dependent on growing in grace. Such a glorious ending is promised to those who build with gold, silver, and precious stones. This is what glorifies God. That was why in the parable of the talents, the one who hid his talent in the ground is punished. He is told, "You wicked and lazy servant" (Matt. 25:26). He does not receive the abundant welcome that his friends obtained who labored and were fruitful. Those who thus labored heard the master say, "Well done, good and faithful servant." They are the ones who got a standing ovation as they entered into the marriage feast of the Lamb.

One of the greatest preachers of the last century, Dr. Martyn Lloyd-Jones, died in 1981. Just before he died, he wrote on a piece of paper for his family the words, "Do not pray for healing. Do not hold me back from the glory."[1] What a testimony! This life is temporary. We all will die. There is a land that is fairer than day. The Father is waiting for us there. Whether we receive a bountiful entrance depends to a large measure on how we are living now. We must grow up to receive such a welcome.

---

1. Iain Murray, *David Martyn Lloyd-Jones: The Fight of Faith, 1939–1981* (Edinburgh: Banner of Truth, 1990), 747.

CHAPTER 20

We Need Reminders about Growing Up

For this reason I will not be negligent to remind you always of these things, though you know and are established in the present truth. Yes, I think it is right, as long as I am in this tent, to stir you up by reminding you, knowing that shortly I must put off my tent, just as our Lord Jesus Christ showed me. Moreover I will be careful to ensure that you always have a reminder of these things after my decease.

—2 PETER 1:12–15

The more I read these words of the apostle Peter, the more I realize that this is the right way to close this book. Peter is emphasizing that we all need to be reminded again and again about the importance of growing up in our spiritual lives. Many who begin their Christian walk look at those whose spiritual lives stand like Mount Everest compared to their own, and they say to themselves, "Oh how I wish I could be like them! I really need to grow." Consequently, they begin to read Christian books and discipline themselves in prayer and Bible reading so they can grow. But then, somewhere down the line, they forget. They become lethargic and complacent in their Christian lives. They begin to live as if the only thing that matters is ending up in heaven rather than hell when this life is over. We all have this downward tendency in us unless we are reminded from time to time about the need to keep on growing until the end of our lives.

Why We Need to Be Reminded

We need continual reminders because we easily forget what we already know. A good example is when you are asked about a practical matter of the Christian faith in a Bible study. You will probably give the right answer even if you do not live out what you are saying. There was a time when you both knew and practiced what is true. But now it is only head knowledge. It is not something you practice anymore. If someone had been reminding you about it, you not only would know it intellectually but also would have continued doing it. The truth is often very well known. The difficulty comes with persevering in it. Thus Peter says, "For this reason I will not be negligent to remind you always of these things, though you know and are established in the present truth."

Peter was not the only one who was fond of reminding the saints. We find the apostle Paul and Jude doing the same. Paul says to the Romans, "Now I myself am confident concerning you, my brethren, that you also are full of goodness, filled with all knowledge, able also to admonish one another. Nevertheless, brethren, I have written more boldly to you on some points, as reminding you, because of the grace given to me by God" (Rom. 15:14–15). To the Corinthians he says, "Moreover, brethren, I declare to you the gospel which I preached to you, which also you received and in which you stand, by which also you are saved, if you hold fast that word which I preached to you—unless you believed in vain. For I delivered to you first of all that which I also received: that Christ died for our sins according to the Scriptures, and that He was buried, and that He rose again the third day according to the Scriptures" (1 Cor. 15:1–4). This was something they should have known as believers, and yet Paul still wanted to remind them of these things. Jude also wrote to believers, saying, "I want to remind you, though you once knew this, that the Lord, having saved the people out of the land of Egypt, afterward destroyed those who did not believe" (Jude v. 5). Even though they fully knew the truth, they had a need to be reminded of it.

We Need Reminders Constantly

We need constant reminders about certain aspects of the Christian faith. The mind functions like the layers of paint in a house. If you have lived in a home for many years and it has been repainted several times, you begin to forget about the original color of paint and are only aware of what you see every day. When you see old photographs, you exclaim, "Oh, I remember now how this house used to look!" Without those photographic reminders, you move on, and the current coat of paint is all you notice or care about. As believers, we must be taken back to that first coat of paint—the first principles of our faith, the foundational indicatives or the things we already have in Christ, and the imperatives of what we must add to our lives so that we might grow to become giants in the faith. We must be reminded of the implications of these things, which results in assurance and stability now and an abundant entrance in heaven in eternity. We need these reminders.

When I was growing up, a lot of homes had wall plaques and signs with Christian messages. These were burned into our memories because every time we looked at the wall we were reminded of those truths. One of them read something like, "Christ is the head of this house, the unseen guest at every meal, the silent listener to every conversation." I would find it on the walls in many homes as I was growing up. I recall thinking to myself that Jesus was listening to every piece of gossip uttered. It helped to keep my mouth shut! These wall plaques were useful reminders. They helped truths to sink down deep into our souls, despite what we are seeing and hearing out there in the world. John Piper refers to one plaque in the home he grew up in. He mentions it in detail in his book *Don't Waste Your Life*. He said that God used it to finally make him focus on glorifying God. The plaque stated, "Only one life, it will soon be past. Only what's done for Christ will last."[1] Imagine growing up seeing a statement like that every day!

---

1. John Piper, *Don't Waste Your Life* (Wheaton, Ill.: Crossway, 2009), 12.

The house I grew up in (which I still live in now) also had an inscription above the front door that read, "But God commends His love to us in this, that while we were still sinners, Christ died for us" (see Rom. 5:8). Every day, whenever I was going out, I would read that statement. As a child I used to wonder what that meant. In due season, it all came back with saving impact when I was converted. I wonder what words are on the walls of your home. I hope it is something that will help you to grow spiritually and to love the Lord your God. If you don't already have inscriptions displayed in your home, a good place to start is the answer to the first question of the Westminster Shorter Catechism, "The chief end of man is to glorify God and enjoy him forever." What a statement worth being reminded of every day! It is easy for us to lose sight of this truth when the world keeps pouring new paint over us. It would be good, after we return home drenched with worldly philosophies, to look up while relaxing or eating or going out the front door and be hit afresh with the truth that life is about glorifying God and enjoying Him forever. We must do something, like Peter, to keep bringing back to our minds the basic principles of the Christian life, because even if we know them, we are prone to forget.

We Need to Be Reminded through Living Preachers

Peter knew that the believers he was writing to needed to be reminded of spiritual truths through the ministry of living preachers: "I think it is right, as long as I am in this tent, to stir you up by reminding you, knowing that shortly I must put off my tent, just as our Lord Jesus Christ showed me" (2 Peter 1:13–14). While Peter was alive, he would keep reminding the saints. We need the ministry of living preachers to stir us up by reminding us of things we easily forget.

What makes living preachers so effective? They are able to see present-day dangers and address them with eternal truth. They can discern what is swallowing the attention of believers today and making them forget how they are supposed to be living. In the days of

Peter, the people of God were under intense persecution. They would easily forget about the vital need for spiritual growth as they were absorbed with how to escape persecution. For most of us today, it is not persecution that is screaming for our attention. At the time of writing this book, some people are so afraid of the coronavirus pandemic that Christian responsibilities and duties have been thrown out the window. Every excuse is given for a lack of commitment. The duty of living preachers is to remind all believers of their responsibilities, even during a pandemic. Similarly, we live in a world of consumerism. The world and its media spew out the same consistent message that a man's life consists of the abundance of his possessions. Hence, so many people are in a rat race for more and more of the world's goods. We are encouraged to chase after things that perish, things that we cannot carry with us into eternity. The world will not remind us that we will soon die, that only what is done for Christ goes with us beyond the grave. This is where living preachers come in. They will remind us to open our eyes so that we can clearly see where our hearts truly are.

Living preachers are also effective because of their strength and intensity. That is why they can stir us up. It is difficult to sense the temperature of Peter's teaching on the written page, although I am sure those who sat and listened to him would remember the warmth and power in his voice as he shared the words the Lord had spoken through him. One of the greatest preachers of the evangelical awakening of the eighteenth century was George Whitefield. When asked to put his sermons into print, he responded, "Aah, but what about the thunder?" There was something in his preaching that could not be caught in a printed sermon.

Another aspect of the living preacher is that he comes from his prayer closet with a message from God. He has loaded the ball and powder into the cannon. When he ignites it, the sin in our hearts is blown apart. We know that it was not our choice to hear that message. It was God who chose to speak to us in the area that we so desperately needed to be addressed.

To gain any benefit from the living preacher, we must deliberately ensure that we are available for the means of grace. One of the most disturbing realities during the COVID-19 pandemic has been that many Christians prefer to relax at home instead of going to church. They prefer using their remote control to choose which preacher they will listen to instead of being at their local church to hear what God has laid on the hearts of their pastors. In the comfort of their homes, they listen to sermons while they do other things. You cannot handle God's truth that way! Unfortunately, that lax attitude has resulted in many spiritual casualties. May God help us to treasure Bible studies, church services, and those moments when there is a living preacher fresh out of his prayer closet with the word of God on his soul. We need it.

We Need to Be Reminded through Departed Preachers

Peter ended with the need for believers to also be reminded through the ministry of departed preachers. He wrote, "Moreover I will be careful to ensure that you always have a reminder of these things after my decease" (2 Peter 1:15). How was he going to do it? By putting it in writing in his epistles. He later wrote, "Beloved, I now write to you this second epistle (in both of which I stir up your pure minds by way of reminder)" (2 Peter 3:1). His goal was that the brethren would be able to remember the things he said to them, even after he was dead.

No doubt, Peter wrote as the Holy Spirit inspired him, but he also made every effort when writing his epistles. It was not as easy as tweeting or posting something on Facebook. He made every effort to plan and pray about what he was going to write to his brethren. The apostles wrote constantly and repetitively with a lot of care because they realized that this was the word of life. They knew it needed to be preserved, reproduced, and passed on from generation to generation long after they had died. Their writings would help the Christian church remain faithful. Their effort continues to bear fruit today as the Bible is available to all of us.

Look at how much Christianity is dependent on being reminded over and over again. I fear the reason why so many Christians are simply existing on autopilot, having little or no impact for Christ, is because they have forgotten Peter's basic message on Christian growth. They hardly bear fruit for the kingdom of God because their attention has been diverted to things that have very little eternal importance. They do not take the time to be reminded.

I join the apostle Peter today to urge you to have God's truths written down where you can see them. Have your Bible in a prominent place where you can read it daily. Ensure that you listen to living and departed preachers regularly. Make every effort to grow up and to continue growing. Keep in mind the price Christ paid for you to bring you to glory. He gave His all. How can you give Him anything less? May this thought cause you to be all the more eager to grow to maturity. Amen!